The future innocense
of the world
& nature remains with our
children
" All Life Matters
Ronald Atkinson
May 2021

REVOLT
Practical Ecology to Save Planet Earth for Our Children

by Rand Atkinson

A.L. Ferndock Publishing LLC

A.L. FERNDOCK PUBLISHING LLC
ISBN: 978-1-63732-182-9
Library of Congress Control Number:
2021903906
Copyright 2021 Rand Atkinson

A.L. Ferndock Publishing LLC
Star Lake, Wisconsin 54561
raferndockpublishng@gmail.com

Printed in the United States of America
By EC Printers, Eau Claire, Wisconsin
Cover Photos by:
A.Hegewald
N. Williams
Adobe Photo Stock
Cover Design by:
Mary Alice Greenan

For Nelli, Ashley, Gracie, Mason, Evie, Morgan
My children and grandchildren who must
confront what mankind is doing to
nature and the land

ACKNOWLEDGEMENTS

Where does one place thanks during a life of challenges and charges? Life is a collective of changes brought on by epiphanies often not recognized during the journey.

My personal road was full of "characters" that both charmed and challenged me to think clearly about what is important. Individuals often inspired by the need to spread the word of Aldo Leopold's Land Ethic. Here are a few: Professor Mike Molitor, Alex Kotovich, Ralph Hopkins, Fran and Fred Hammerstrom, Leon Johnson, Bob Schave, Bob Hansis, Tom Meier, Bob Ellingson, Robert Wendt, Lowell Klessig, Phil Lewis Jr., and Bill Genszler. Many are now gone, but I hope their passions to change the way we physically treat nature and their optimism that we must change our ways to be humans as part of the land will prevail.

The bridge between past and present is the . secret to the future. The aboriginal, indigenous, and woodsmen ways of living with the land must be understood and dispensed by environmental educators to all ages and races. Those that understand the importance of these ways must become future leaders who will make decisions that preserve and protect the natural world. I thank those who do this in advance.

My dear thanks go to my children, Nelli Williams and Ashley Hegewald who inspire all around them to be ethical towards the land. I thank Mary Alice Greenan for her digital abilities and patience to bring this all together.

Contents

Part 2: Out of Step

Part 3: To Get in Step for Our Children

REVOLT

Practical Ecology to Save Planet Earth for Our Children

Preface

It was in the 1970's when the environmental movement began that I was introduced to the teachings of Aldo Leopold through a professor, a student of one of his graduate students. Leopold's passions and philosophy had been passed from professor to student to professor to student, again and again. Though land resource related problems and human impacts have grown exponentially from 1940's his message still rings clear to every new situation regarding Leopold's precious land.

I was told that Leopold required writing courses in the curriculum of his graduate students. They knew the special importance of his words and philosophy must be heard, understood, and spread throughout the world. The prominence of his words has been perceived and carried forward into an environmental movement, conservation preservation efforts, and laws. Though he foresaw our predicament of this failing earth and knew the reasons why, he still had hope we could shift our values to see land as a community not as a commodity.

During these 1970's college days we used to have conversations on what will save the "land". Will it be Leopold's Land Ethic or environmental laws? For the last forty years we have witnessed many laws passed that have helped to save the land, but as with greed and politics it is man's cultural ethics in the long run that are important to life.

These essays are an attempt to bring Aldo's wisdom and advice to today's culture. These writings are plain and straight forward, not poetic as Aldo, but simple endeavors to address what has come about since his time. These essays were composed during a 40-year career that was incessantly and passionately engaged with the land and natural resources. This is my fate on excepting the land ethic.

These essays are narratives of what one can do to make a difference. Written for the common person ... hopefully the thinking human who knows their offspring will be confronting many life destroying events, circumstances, and realities our own species and too many other species must face if we do not change our ways globally.

Forward

Over the years, I have read Leopold's *Sand County Almanac* so many times, but not enough. Each time gleaning ...at first knowledge, then inspiration, then wisdom, then all repeated with each passing year. This book is truly a creation for all time to those who listen and those who do not. It is time for all to listen. It is time for REVOLT.

Aldo literally called for a REVOLT-"revolt against the tedium of the merely economic attitude towards the land". It has come to the point where the "land" as Aldo called this planet's earth living presence, whether land, water, or air, needs to be understood, appreciated, AND paid attention to. We are at that critical point where this economic attitude will destroy the existence of the ecological communities and natural systems that supports all life.

This book is about this necessary REVOLT. It is about the history of what man has done with the land ... with nature since Leopold's writing. Part 1 gives examples of the capabilities and value to spirit and thought of being on the land in each season. Part 2 describes the misdeeds that a mere economic attitude has done and continues to do to the land and the plight of our planet if it continues. Part 3 defines, simply, what it will take to change man's destruction and move to a sustainable planet earth. This book is about a revolution and uprising that must occur to save us from ourselves.

Humility

Life has no meaning without humbleness ... the humbleness of place, of the moment, and of the trust in the self that the subconscious brings to reality.

At one moment one is secure in the presence of shelter and the routine of this physical world whether it be family and friends, laughter or pleasure, and solemn song or dance. The next moment we long for the change in this same world towards adventure and conflict, power, need for more, and the freedom from of the routine of the security of a rigid dance lesson. The conscious mind powers us towards the false reality of humanity that is the only game in town. There has been no humbleness.

So, to see the truth we must leave town to seek a home within while we leave this security of the known towards a country of uncertainty. We drive into the blizzard where the snowflakes fill the pathway with a white road of nothingness. Life slows and becomes black or white, tracks end beyond the visibility of our new view. This is humility.

Part 1: LESSONS OF SEASONS

WINTER

December Frost

There is a time between the brown grayness of late fall and the white bleakness of snowy winter that creates a blended contrast of both. It is a time when fog has penetrated the freezing night. It is a time in the civilized world where at night the frost forms on your windshield despite the full blasting of the defrost system and travel is indeed perilous with the encompassing fog and the dampening cold on the road before you.

In the natural world there is a reverse of the earlier frost that hugged the valleys while leaving the hillside as a brown tone photo. Now all hillside vegetation is white as an arctic winter and the valley brown as the coat of a fall whitetail deer. The fog and frost have combined to give eeriness to distance and the perception of it.

That stand of trees that had a background of a grassy brown hillside now becomes a misty silhouette standing alone in broken white against pure white gray. Every hillside shrub or blade of grass is covered with thick frost giving each a stark skeleton of pure white.

On closer inspection each blade of grass on the hillside that before blended into those stems in front and back now stand as individuals with their own personality as if you were looking through a magnifying glass at the details that separate them. Those that had their terminal seed heads to browsing deer or eaten by birds can easily be identified from the neighboring stem of who still have a flocculent bounty. The detail of the past deadly frost of fall now gives individual plants meaning to its place in time and space.

Crows are creatures that are never caught by surprise because of their keen eyesight and guarded nature; but add a fog frost and you are surely going to catch them in a scavenging haunt. The white frosted trees, shrubs, and grasses blending their white coats into the fog of both land and sky. The black contrast of crows and their caw in the misty silence disturbs this eerie calm.

Human structures seem out of place on such days. The frost glazing does not thicken as on those things of nature. Their squared edges and mass again contrast the foggy mood. Even the old poled-wooden bird house stands out like an abandoned pioneer home on a vast prairie of nothingness.

Even the birds that move across this frozen landscape, dashing between cover and food sources, are confused. Yet, they quickly discover in the first feeding of morning that this sparkly frost can be shaken off on the first peck of investigation. This hard December frost is not as crucial to our feathered fellows' survival as a late winter ice storm; this frost is gone by midday and the fatty seed of fall is still hangs on its skeleton.

North of January

When the frigid nights carry their lowest temperatures into the days for weeks on end, we know this as January. When the late rising sun finally crawls over the east hillside to reveal its power to the bitter cold landscape, and the hawk perches high in a tree so its dark feathers can gain another minute bit of warmth from the early morning glow, we know this as January. Eventually, the bitter night gives way to another day in which the survival of the fit will be tested.

Because the fire of the wood stove has died in the night, the cabin dweller moves quickly from warm bed to clothing, and he know this as January. When he opens the quilted blinds to the morning brightness to see the crystalline frost painted on the windowpanes, he knows this as January.

After an hour of reviving coals to add heat and coaxing the teakettle on the wood stove to whistle, he knows this as January. When the laundry is hung, steaming, on the clothesline on the front porch, it stiffens in moments to cardboard cloth; when the breeze taps the frozen cloth against a porch post until it becomes a free sail again, he knows this as January.

When he thinks about what is important in life and this question enters the cabin dweller's mind, "Is the wood pile high enough to last the winter?" He knows this as January. When he abandons the reverie and acts on the question accepting the need, he enters the bright day to split the section of stump left to freeze for this occasion, knowing fully that this is January.

The frozen ants fall from the split stump, he knows the juncos and chickadees waiting for the late morning warmth will scurry from one wind-ruffled brush to the next and will find delight in these frozen ants.

When the dweller peers down the valley from the cabin and sees the shadowed tracks of a deer, he knows that it has survived and seeks food and shelter on this peaceful haven of land. The coyote pack, seeking the deer, wishes for deeper snow for the same reason that the deer wishes for less.

To say you have survived a lifetime of winters through the knowledge that your forebearers gained over time is revealed ... an understanding realized in the quietness of this long month. The cabin dweller wonders if our modern culture can ponder this same wisdom to understand the intricacies of nature and make decisions that will preserve it for all the Januarys to come.

Can modern technology-oriented man achieve that miracle and appreciate both the labors of our past and the simplicity that brings happiness to the winter soul?

Interaction Ecology

One can spend years living near nature and only glimpse at its complexities. Yet simple understandings of life histories of only a few animals can be rewarding in understanding how interconnected those of us that live on Planet Earth are. Man's activities beyond his origins as hunter and gathers have influenced these intricacies severely. The sooner we understand what we have done to the land, the better decisions we can make regarding what is right.

Studies of the winter landscape, that often appears lifeless, have found that activity under the snowpack thrives from bacteria to rodents to predators. The three rodents that live there have their own separate food source: the mice eat seeds, the voles graze on grass, and the shrews devour insect eggs and larva. Sometime these separate species are communal and probably consume each other's food. Their waste is combined with the leaf litter tissue broken down by freezing and thawing and soon will be providing nutrients to the warming soil of spring.

Slim weasels can enter these snow tunnel homes, but few other predators manage to find them unless the tunnels surface near tree trunks, where winter sun shining on these dark surfaces opens an entrance for them. Then foxes, coyotes, martens, and bobcats seek these tunnels for unwary rodents that are drawn to the increased heat. The winter food chain of rodent prey has shifted from that of the open ground flying predators of the owls, hawks, and kestrels to these hungry winter mammals.

In this example alone, we can visualize the interactions of several species that shift from season to season. Changes in weather such as the durations and amounts of snowfall or rain are balanced in nature through intertwined food chains. But human disturbances that cause specie and habitat loss can mean death in the food web. Shifts in the food web can accommodate some change, yet the continued climate changes induced by humans can have serious effects on these long-established ecosystems.

Disease and Survival

After the coldest night of the winter the sun slowly rises in the east, eventually bringing a little warmth to mid-winter mornings. As the bright midday sun gives way to a colder afternoon a coyote appears on the hillside of valley south of the cabin. He scampers to and fro, vigorously nosing the ground hoping to surprise a deer mouse or vole. I see it has but a rod of a tail. The ravages of mange make this hunting trip even more important, as the warmth received from the sustenance of this day must replace the warmth lost from a furry tail that curls around his body this upcoming cold night.

He continues his mission until he reaches the base of the opposite hillside where I suspect he has found some frozen carcass a crow had found earlier in the day. He ravishingly chews the remaining meat and pulls his head up every minute or so to sniff the air for danger. His hunger and the deep cold have brought him out into the day light, and this pause in his travel makes him an easy target to the aim of humans. A plane flies over, again his head pops up from the carcass, he quickly glances at the sky, pinpoints the sound, and returns to the scavenged success. Only a few minutes pass before he again sniffs the winds and now meanders southeast out of the grasslands of the field to the cover of the steep-hilled forest.

Native Americans call the coyote the song dog. Their belief is that when all life perishes on Earth ... the song dog will survive. The question is "Will he survive the diseases and habitat destruction brought on by the modern societies of humans".

Snow Country

Today brought a new experience of snow. I have not really paid close attention to snow for many years, maybe since I was a child. But now, as time repeats itself through the ages with a twist, my time this winter with snow is a reprise of youth when you had the free time to pay attention. By now one should have wisdom that adds to its wonder.

Today was a day where spring thaw began after a long winter in the Northwoods. The snow came in late October and just keep on coming. There was a short thaw a few days in early January, but deep in the woods where the sun does not shine it was hardly noticed. The snowbanks along a plowed forest road were piled high and the road so narrowed it became a tunnel. In places it became an old-covered bridge with snow-laden pine boughs as the roof. On late mornings, when the winter wind was able to penetrate the deep woods the accumulated snow in the boughs above would fall with hollow thud ... unheard but by a solemn mind.

The business and exercise of snow removal from a walkway or driveway path was always interrupted by a look skyward where the snowfall came to rest on the pine tree limbs. In the northern forest of conifers or pines, without the wind the snow accumulates in the canopy, especially when the snowfall is light and often like this year.

This snowfall accumulation on the long branches of white and red pines that extend from the trunk bends them towards the ground. The more open grown pines that have lower limbs that are still alive with needles bend to the ground creating a teepee like shelter beneath. If you squint and look at the landscape of pines, it resembles a panorama of snow-capped mountains.

The snow is so deep around these pines now these teepees become shelters for many creatures of the Northwoods. It is no wonder that on winters with deep snow such as this, deer eventually find shelter in the cedar swamps of conifers where the cedar, the only palatable needle of pine can offer both food and shelter. Even then, during the worst of winters these last resort areas become graveyards for the whitetail but survival food for the now restored population of hungry wolf predators. Death brings life to another.

The winter thaw comes, and the winter landscape changes. The now crusted snow had both predator and prey walking on top of the snow and the hunting, feeding, and hiding strategies change. Now 10-12 deer bed each night around the cabin. They disperse in different directions as singles or small family groups as morning breaks. After a long winter of concentrated browsing of shrub brush adjacent to deep paths through the snow this dispersal means browsing shrub buds in other areas now more accessible with snow melt.

The snow is finally giving away to the warmer temperatures and rain. The fog and damp cold of twenty degrees at night gives way to a cold thirty something degree hard rain the next afternoon. Walking down the short drive on slick ice was nearly impossible but the rest of the walk south down Star Lake Road to Snyder Lake Road was nearly clear of any ice ... any sign of wolf tracks of the long winter has vanished. Deer are now browsing on exposed patches of old grass and are now bedding on the same bare places saving all their remaining energy. When I returned in the heavy afternoon rain, two deer standing under two large white pines 100 feet away did not move. The effects of the long winter snow are framed skeleton silhouettes of the beings that lived through it.

The history of the winter's snowfall has been exposed in the thaw. The wood ashes placed on the drive and walkway during the early thaw but covered by more snowfall are now imbedded in dark ice that draws the sun's heat and turns it to slush. Yet, it is the view of the natural areas beneath pines that gets your attention. The low snow-covered pine limbs now silently drip rain through the fog. This is pine tree country, one small aspect of the Northwoods; but the salvation of the whitetail for both food, shelter and a warmer ground for bedding ... and I am sure for other animals including their wolf predators.

Spring Thaw

When the sun gains the strength to pull your winter coat from your shoulders; the reminder of the winter's past activities begins to draw forms upon the landscape. We begin to awake from the winter daze of the slowed time and glacial indifference.

You now can put the snowshoes and skis away and walk about without them. But they are not forgotten as the paths you now walk are the same. As the snow melts down to the crust that now supports you, one can see the layer that reveals the ski paths you took from November on. If you wait a few more days, each snowshoe adventure in January becomes clear. If you cannot quite see the path, a suddenly crusted snow collapses beneath you, bringing you to your knee; you have stepped off the old path onto untrodden and uncompacted snow.

Soon you seek to follow where there is no snow. When the thermometer temperature barely climbs to the daily thaw, the south slopes know it is time for spring. But you remember that on the dry and poor soils of this farm; the same summer sun on this slope begs for the shade of a trees.

Next, the snow receded from the north edge of the field. The pattern of the winter snowstorms is clear now, the trees along this edge were a wind break to drop the drifting snow a few yards away in the field. But the trees and boulders now serve spring by soaking up and reflecting heat to melt the snow at its edge. It was a long winter and those small mammals that survived till now must wonder why they chose this north slope of rock and boulder to hibernate among. It is evident now as you find the normally scurrying chipmunk perched on the largest rock trying to get the first heat of the day – it has survived the winter here, but the rock shelter of growing season is more important for it to escape the sly fox that dens on the south slope.

It is along this tree line that the whitetail deer now ventures, absorbing the heat of the late winter sun and protected by trees from blistery north wind. All winter this field forest edge also provided food for them. The buds of any shrub or tree within their browse reach was now missing.

Late winter and spring fog in the morning is inevitable. The cold white earth and the warming air are as confused as you as you peer through an existence that blends what is beneath with what is above. A flattened trumpet sound pierces the silent milky air; the sandhill cranes bugle their fog horns to find their way out through this vast sea of lowland. When the morning sun gains enough momentum to break the eastern horizon, it instantly turns the frost on the east facing tin roof to a warming drip. The daily thaw has begun.

SPRING

Agriculture and the Bear

Life in southwest Wisconsin is driven by the agricultural industry Its infrastructure permeates both the city and country, through a childhood working on the farm, through the agricultural colleges, to a funeral in the country church cemetery. The heart of the best farmland in Wisconsin lies both north and south of Platteville in Grant County where the tall grass prairie laid sod and good earth all around. This soil is so good for agriculture that barely a remnant of the prairie vegetation is left that made it what it is. Only a few creek's meander through the grain fields where a hybridized raccoon might travel to the next grain bin; the water in the creek is not a travel lane as much as source of water that it needs for its lack of saliva glands needed for eating.

This corn country is like the rest of the former tall grass prairies of the upper Midwest. Climatologists have recently reported that the corn crop of this area now effects the climate of the region. Industrial agriculture and genetic engineering of corn has enabled the leaves to be wider and the rows planted closer together. This in return has the ability in July and August to raise the relative humidity through the process of plant transpiration. This transfer of water into the atmosphere over such a large area of crops has now cooled the climate. During the dog days of summer, when temperatures often climb into the 90's or into the 100's in the past, will seldom be witnessed again. Yet the increased humidity in the 80's will make summer heat still miserable. If modern technology in agriculture can change climate how soon will history repeat the turning a land of milk and honey into a desert?

Enter the wild black bear. How this black bear, absent from the southwest Wisconsin landscape for a hundred years found its way to the village of Livingston may never be explained; except bird feeders that have replaced the prairie seeds that once fed birds and the over produced and over wrapped spoiled food in garbage cans was food for a resourceful and territorial- seeking hungry bear. The reaction of the people of Livingston was just a follow-up of the asteroid that fell nearby a few months before, but it was as if an alien species had chosen Livingston to visit.

The gossip of the presence of a bear spread faster than butter on hot sweet corn. Soon a line of cars was following the poor bear. The cars were soon joined by the state patrol as now a public safety threat was being witnessed upon the land. Ironically, the chased bear sought the country and the biggest tree it could find; It might have been a burr oak remnant of the tall grass prairie savanna; it was in fact, a lonely tree in the middle of cornfield owned by the corn genetic giant Monsanto. The cars blocked the country road as the patrolman observed the excitement; but now trespass law was in effect as those with cameras ventured to the base of the tree. The traffic to the tree through the corn was too much to "bear", and soon the Monsanto corn was in jeopardy and the land was posted. Still the cell phone stalkers persisted until darkness which brought a welcome protection and a new type of loneliness to the bear's existence.

Why? Are the primordial thoughts of our hunter and gather genetics starved for the experience of the wild on their way to the agricultural epitome of Monsanto's enzyme-filled corn? Are we so starved for a natural experience after being surrounded by corn for the last three quarter of a century? Does the bear represent the last vestige in this country of what is right on the landscape?

After this mishap, I am sure this bear will seek the more forested areas of this county. This year's wet and early spring will provide a massive berry crop to fill his belly, while Monsanto's corn fills ours with corn syrup and acid reflux. In the fall, once the berries are gone and the bear returns to the cornfields to fill his belly with a wide swath of now ripe genetic corn, I hope citizens blame it on the raccoons not the poor bear who may have the ability to survive much longer on the landscape than us.

And now you must be asking what is a hybrid raccoon? Long before genetic engineering of corn, and long before one had an understanding what was truly conservation, the fur trappers in the early days of the twentieth century in Wisconsin brought raccoons from Missouri. You see even those close to the land as a trapper and hunters made mistakes in the name of profit. The fur market for raccoon coats and hats paid much more for the darker pelts of racoons found in Missouri than the blonde pelts from Wisconsin.

Responding to this price difference, Missouri raccoons were brought to Wisconsin. They hybridized and the darker colored coats are now more prevalent. Very rarely does one find a racoon that wears a blonde coat. With this highbred also came more aggressive behavior and reproductive vigor. This high bred vigor and continuous foraging close to wetlands and waterways decimated healthy populations of turtles, frogs, and crayfish.

Today, the term "habitat destruction" is a common term we use for reasons for loss of diversity. We fail to understand the process of what it is. We need to not only consider man's history on the land but the natural history of land itself and its original species before the influences and mistakes of the human species.

Forest Spring

Spring is approaching summer in the Northwoods. Daily walks down sand and gravel roads changed from a steady walk to using a faster bicycle to outpace the mosquitos, yet the timing of several hatches of different species of dragonflies from area waters seemed to be timed to reduce mosquito numbers. Tracks of wolves, coyotes, and foxes on new winter snow have been replaced by those in the sand. With the coming of spring, sandhill cranes and black bear tracks have been added to the list. The occasional animal track could be identified and followed giving hints to a moment in time for local mammals and birds.

Often, you find fresh animal scat that was not present the day before and often it can be used and combined with tracks to identify the animal. Yet the discovery one makes from traveling at the speed of a cruising bicycle are that butterflies congregate on the scat!

As the spring warmed there has been a progression of butterfly eruptions, just like the dragonflies. This is particularly evident along the forested road where butterflies seem to be drawn by the openness and the faster daily warming on a sunny day. Each butterfly specie eruption utilizes the fresh scat and often congregates can be found in rain puddles on the roads that pass-through low-lying areas.

One morning four species of butterfly were utilizing a large mammal scat pile with the most recent butterfly specie eruption being dominate. Was it wolf or bear, two species remnants of the wilderness? One must marvel and wonder at the ecology of connection and diversity there is between the wolf or bear and so many species of butterflies? Is there a nutrient or mineral so scarce in this pine barrens that this concentrated waste pile of a species of mammal would be important to a family of insects? Then there are more questions to be answered: of a road that was not here before humans created it; the increased heat of the sun reaching earth; and the need for nutrients as waste returning to the earth?

SUMMER

August Morning

It may be a bit harder to wake up early at this cabin in August. Few birds sing you awake except for the cardinal and mourning dove with their hope of a second nesting. They know it has been a good year with plenty of summer moisture to produce food for a second brood.

Yet after a storm in the night, that quieted all voices with wind and thunder, the creatures of the night again spoke. The water levels in the pond recovered after Saturday's storm and even more after last nights' rain.

The green frog praised such event or was hopeful the sound of rain on the landscape brought woeful mates from the adjacent woods. His occasional washtub-base croak penetrates the night from dusk to dawn.

The tree frogs that occupy the hillsides adjacent to the pond will not be satisfied with occasional calls; their song is more continuous maybe because the distance and number of perching females is more than a hop away. Maybe this wet year confuses them or provides them false hope. The lush vegetation growth is a signal to the tree frog that there is more habitat for his offspring, especially if the future of this land for his chorus is guaranteed; if this land is free from grazing, rain events keep water in the pond, and the owner keeps the mortgage up to date.

Waking before first light also provides the last aerial dances of our feeding bats. At dusk last evening they left their cabin slumber chamber. With a few turns around the cabin to make sure their fellow dancers were joining them, they disappeared for the evening. I suspect perhaps the new pond ballroom is by now producing emerging insects. At first light they return to circle around the cabin again before going to roost in the cracks of the cabin.

Knowing the bat and frog night feeding reduced the mosquitoes, this proud owner of the land knew he could hike through the woods this morning with a lesser threat of getting bit!

Coyote Castle

This first walk through the property about to be mine awed my soul when I found a few open-grown bur oaks old enough to have witnessed the prairie and its fires before man brought his plow. Equally impressive were the open- and closed-canopy grown white oak I found. In my musing, they seemed to say, " We were the kings who ruled the woods after the plow stopped the fires." But the rich soil beneath also gave an abundance of black walnut—enough to create the dark forest of my unconscious mind.

I had been seeking a piece of land for nearly a year when I found it on that Friday afternoon. During that year I visited many hilly sites of field and forest but found none with what I was seeking—a true forest, a forest that had outlived the tests of time; fire, storm, and wind, but lacked the acts of man with his saw, cow, or plow.

From the town road I could see the well-developed hardwood canopy and a few towering white pines that reminded me of the Northwoods. A walk revealed what my subconscious knew all along: here was a place where man's effort to claim nature's resources had faltered. Thirteen acres out of seventy-seven acres had somehow survived as a healthy hardwood forest patch.

The canopied woods and rich soil beneath led me to think of water, the third element I would need. The realtor knew his prospective buyer. "There is a spring on the property that a buyer can dam to build a pond," he said.

The full story of this valley had not yet been told, but some clues remained to be pieced together by observation. A tight valley fell from the open contoured farmland above into my now prized woods. At the top of this narrow-wooded valley a small spring emerged, and 50 yards later a second slightly larger one. It appeared at that moment that enough water had flowed over time to expose and smooth the limestone bed to create a few three-foot waterfalls. The small springs soon entered the open meadow of the valley floor and disappeared. Yet for hundreds of yards down the valley remnant banks and gullies could be found in the thick grassland.

The larger valley witnessed many a storm and spring runoff before the contoured fields above and the growth of the forest canopy on the hillside protected it. At one time, heavy rains eroded silt from the plowed fields and cattle had grazed on the steep hillsides, so no forest canopy would develop there. Some old farmers had protected this small narrow valley and hilltop for some reason. Perhaps, I mused, when he was a child exploring the wild, away from the chores of a farm, it was in this glen that he found solitude and adventure, then as an adult, chose to fence the cattle out.

On my way back to the truck I tried to visualize a winding path for a new road through the woods that would not disturb this unique site too much. Then I found another clue to the history of this land; a volcano castle of bare mineral soil erupting over 30 feet on the forest floor. Instantly, I smelled the musk of coyote, which brought an old olfactory memory of deer hunting in a damp cedar swamp where this same odor was carried on the air signaling the coyote's approach.

This coyote family's home has been here for decades without notice. This coyote castle, reeking of longevity, still stands not a hundred yards from the cabin and even closer to the road that travels to it.

This coyote den had probably been used for centuries and perhaps by other Wisconsin mammals. It is possible that the master digger, the badger, at one time had a hand in building this den when fire, prairie, and the open-grown bur oak could be seen from this pyramid. In this narrow, spring valley the den would provide refuge from the fires in the prairie above and below. A badger is the heavy weightlifter of the prairie, the coyote the sprinter away from the fire.

On a good year, a coyote female can litter nineteen pups: a year lean of mice and rabbits, only one. The young must be fed and nurtured for six to nine months by foraging the night away. With more pups at the castle door the female and pack members would have to forage during the riskier day. In the fall male pups would disperse from the territory and the females would then make up the local pack helping raise the next years young in this castle.

The coyote is mature at a year and lives on for ten. One can easily imagine a female coyote, and then her female offspring for generations, returning to this castle den as the oak forest emerged and grew to shade the den. The song dog has survived the fire, the plow, the cow, and the gun.

To understand who you are and where you belong always comes with a sense of place over time. Adaptation to change points to continual survival of self, offspring, and place. There will be a long-lived place for man too ... if he understands and cares for the land.

Summer Hail

On Friday evening the "hailstorm of the century" cut a wide path through the landscape of southwest Wisconsin. This wind driven hail from the north at nearly a 45-degree angle did incredible damage to personal possessions. House siding and roofs, sky lights and windows, air conditioners, and of course, the American icon … the automobile.

Crop damage was extensive as the length of the blast of quarter size projectiles lasted nearly 10 minutes or more. Much of the corn was at the stage of pollination with the top tassel being shredded and its pollen eliminated. I was told that until pollination occurs the nitrogen levels in the stock and leaves is so high that it would be toxic to farm animals if green chopped and fed to them. The corn hybrid of today's wide leaf was genetically created for photosynthesis and fast growth not for pulverizing hail.

The real landscape, the land, the natural one, never was a news item, as nature itself quietly went about adjusting to the phenomena it had faced before. Those leaves and branches of this year's new grow at the top of the trees were shredded and released to the ground. My road through the woods was literally paved with stemmed leaves of the canopy trees. As I look at treetops two weeks later from the lofted deck of my cabin all that remains are the broken stems with a few tattered leaves silhouetted in the morning sun.

Where the hail did not meet the tree canopy the plunge into the landscape continued. Many developing fruits of the walnut, oak, and hickory were loosened, and in delayed action are now dislodged from their nutrient source and fall to the ground. How will this affect the survival of the young squirrels? Did these penetrating bombs of hail disrupt or destroy the second nesting of many bird species? If a parent bird sat on its nest what a bruising it might have taken; yet it seems a norm that most woodland and orchard birds chose tree and shrub limb crotches for their nest fortified from such a rare event. Will a tree dendrologist or sawyer note the 2009 glitch in the growth of the tree rings when the time comes? I expect that man will forget this storm in the woods.

As one reaches the edge of the woods the trees give way to shrubs. The hails force continues to damage leaf and twig but extends to sun ripening berries, wild plums, choke cherries, and immature nuts. Will these be enough to support both birds and mammals through the upcoming fall and winter? For two days after the storm the avian songs of my cabin's field and forest were not sung or dropped to a murmur. Where the hailstorm was the talk of media and the street corner it appeared the mourning of nature's loss was more reverent.

A return to the meadow and restored prairie that was not in crops revealed another subtle wondering of how nature must respond. Many flowers or forbes of this natural world are in blossom during this time of late July and hail was not specific in which plant it decided to affect. The flowers with the wide-topped blossoms often had the stem ripped from the rest of the crown. Wide-leaved flowers, such as the common milkweed seemed especially decimated both in flower and leaf structure. Yet it is related and rarer red or marsh milkweed with narrower leaves seemed to escape with only one of three or four wide topped blossom stems severed. Both milkweeds I have observed for years as they are necessary plants for monarch butterfly survival. Both are host plants for egg laying, caterpillar larva feeding, and adult butterfly nectar feeding. Yet the red milkweed is twice or three times the choice for egg-laying than the common milkweed when available. For this very choice one cannot help but believe that nature, including hail over eons of time, made it this way for the survival of the monarch.

Are there other intricacies of nature that we do not see but need to observe and understand? A need to understand nature has never been more important than now when manmade changes in climate bring drastic changes in weather that can affect the landscape that has existed for thousands of years. Pay attention!

Sunday Morning Economy

After the scorching days through the summer solstice the mood of these cabin woods has changed. Through this heat the birds of this hilltop woke at the hint of light and intensely declared territory and songs of perhaps a second nesting. It lasted no longer than a half hour and by 8 am their morning foraging was complete. These woodland birds, just as humans, move towards shade, instinctively some place cool and quiet, away from the day's mounting heat.

Yesterday's fast-moving thunderstorms brought in the night a cold front that aroused a rare summer cool north wind. This morning's bird revelry came slower and with less intense vigor. Each species of bird: the cardinal, indigo bunting, oriole, phoebe, and robin had their own soliloquies, as if knowing this was Sunday morning and that the partitioning of time was not driven by a schedule to 'beat the heat'.

This was the morning of the birds. As light increased, I found both cardinals and orioles skittering haphazardly through the rogue orchard adjacent to the cabin feeding on the insects slowed down by the cool night. So near, the cycle of life was unfolding before me.

The lightning bugs for the last several weeks shared the night sky creating twinkling stars above and below the horizon. The moisture of winter and timely rain of spring brought abundant plant growth and heavy sweet laden fruit to the mulberry and apple trees that in return drew insects. This morning these insects have drawn birds feeding themselves and their earlier hatched young. Before long, the ripened fruit will feed both insects and birds. But today the birds stake claim over the insect kingdom.

The prairie in front of the cabin gains from the adjacent rogue orchard, and vice versa. The timing and intricacies of nature is never more pronounced as spring advances into summer. The blossoms of trees give way to the blossoms of the prairie. The bees and butterflies that are drawn to the sweet odor of fruit in the orchard are also drawn to the bright colors of the orange butterfly milkweed, the red milkweed, the yellow coreopsis, and the purple prairie clover. Pollination and nectar production become factions in the natural economy of ecology. Can we learn from such a morning? These simple complexities of nature are made to sustain us if we are willing to be a part of it rather than its master.

Sunday School

Today's rain was predicted yesterday as a solid line of storms stretched from Texas to Nebraska to Iowa heading towards Wisconsin. To know that it is going to rain for sure on Sunday- a day that leaves more options than the rest of the week- gives one a chance to ponder the world about us. Yesterday the wind blew from the west and then south. As evening approached the high clouds shielded the August sun and the day's humidity fled. And as suddenly as these changes occurred by nightfall the air calmed, and stillness set in. Today's parade of weather came too quickly to fully cool the cabin's interior.

The daylight summer's deep green foliage gave way to darkness, with it came the chorus of crickets and solos from various tree frogs. In Wisconsin, the spring months of May and June are the wet months, and July and August are typically our hot dry months.

But this year, 2009, brought an opposite pattern that delayed blossoms, slowed down the insect population, and created even a greener landscape for these summer months.

Well before dawn, the rain on this cabin's tin roof began its wind driven beat. It quickly changed to the beat of steady rain, then to climatic crescendos as the storm center passed, and eventually died to silence as the rain stopped. The few summer birdsongs that remained piped in as the low clouds and rainy skyline replaced sunrise with a dim morning light.

The rain again blew in gusts from the west and south trying to decide a second time which front to assault this new day – and then again, a calm set in. I took advantage of this to walk up my driveway of woods and meadow to the rustic road. The sky parted blue, and my pace met my mood of hope and direction.

Distantly visible in the haze I viewed for the first-time multiple pillars of silos on the farthest horizon. They appeared as the city of Oz through the field of poppies. How ironic, this summer's severe corn destroying hail made the blue monoliths of this farm country either brighter or useless. My line of sight shifted to the silhouettes of a few open grown bur oaks that had witnessed both prairie and fire and now witnesses what the plow can do to nature. With this summer's hail, nature won this round of earthly challenges.

As I walked further down the road, the activities of a waning summer were now creating another contrast. The fence line shrubs sprayed by the town patrolman left veined skeletons of the remaining plants. The normally red sumac now was black against a green pasture. A patch of intertwined bittersweet and Virginia creeper vines chasing up a box elder tree showed the mixed result of the chemical onslaught with the bittersweet surviving and the creeper dying. As the cards were dealt in this rural landscape of field and forest, nearly every tree has Virginia Creeper racing towards its crown, but there are few bittersweets to reflect orange beads into the fall season. When do shrubs become "brush" to be sprayed?

I looked to the south and west again. I saw darkness and the wind began to push the rain from the east. My pace changed to a race against the rain. It slanted from the east until trees lining the road on both sides guided the wind, so rain now fell vertically. Approaching an open field, the rain altered again from the east to the south before giving up to a drizzle.

In the woods of my driveway, the canopy of the oaks and walnuts had delayed this recent shower enough to bring raindrops down slowly, quelling the storm surges into a more gentle and quieter pitter-patter. I hope these altering periods of wind and light clouds to driving rain and darkness continue all day, so humbleness to the greatness of nature and the safety of my woods cabin cannot be taken for granted.

The Why of Japanese Beetles

Japanese beetles, *Popillia japonica*, have spread westward from New Jersey since it was discovery in 1916. By 1972 infestations covered twenty-two states east of the Mississippi plus Iowa and Missouri. Few know that it is also the most widespread turf grass pest in the United States.

We are appalled at this beetle's ability in the adult stage to completely devour the leaf tissue of a plant but fail to reason as to why they are so abundant. This insect targets diseased and poorly nourished plants, shrubs, and trees. Often the plants they choose are poorly adapted to our geography.

Their eggs are laid in the ground in late summer, and the hatched small white larva, called grubs that feed on the roots of grasses, sometimes killing it. They spend the next ten months of the year in this larva stage in the ground. After feeding through late fall, they burrow into the soil deeper than the frost and remain inactive all winter. In early spring they feed on the turf root until late spring when become plant feeding beetles, again.

Effective control or elimination of the adult beetles we see feeding on many of our ornamental flowers, shrubs, and trees as well as the larval grubs we do not see beneath our lawn turf is not working. When USDA researchers studied the life cycle of the Japanese beetle, they found the natural diseases and predators that would limit their reproduction and success during their ten months underground are no longer present in the soils of the urban landscape of lawns and ornamental plants. Reintroduction of these diseases and parasitic organisms has been their suggested solution along with the application of ineffective pesticides and trapping above ground. All above and below the ground control methods appear to be ineffective and expensive.

The ethical answers to the control of these invasive beetles are to: maintain a healthy soil without pesticides; reduce the area of lawn in our yards; and replace foreign cultivators and ornamental plants with native species. With these new practices our urban landscape can better relieve the stresses on nature and our cultural world has wrought.

Returning the soil to its natural state will restore the parasitic organisms and bacteria that will kill the larva. Taking away the sod that the larva "grubs" feed on will reduce their food source in both fall and spring. Increasing native plants on the landscape will also limit their adult food source and provide a natural diversity of species that will in turn increase competition.

All these methods for control are logical, healthy, and safe ways to deal with the Japanese beetle. The world of nature will again begin functioning sustainably.

Passing of the Northwoods

A late summer visit to the Northwoods generated memories of a decade ago spent studying the lake country. The first day of the visit was a continuous cold rain of the late summer- welcome after a long dry but cool summer. This country has changed since my earlier time here; there was more development and people. So far, the lakes and woods are still resilient to human development. An early morning rising reveals just that.

Walking out the cabin door to the towering red oaks and pines on the south shore of Plum Lake the call of the pileated woodpecker broke the dewy morning silence. Above me I noticed the pioneer white birches on their last legs scattered among in the oaks. On each leafless topped birch were large holes, the signature of this king of the woodpeckers. The rhythmic writing continued until another ancient call from another pileated woodpecker broke its' concentration and it moved on to a second dying birch top. I am pleased to find that this species still thrives in these recent disturbances. Yet when the birches are replaced by red oaks and more pines, they may have to adjust their territories to the young forest stands in other parts of the Northern Highlands.

Moving down to the lakefront, the signs of the approaching fall and dry summer were evident. Shrubs beneath the forest canopy were already turning pale with a few grape and Virginia creeper vines showing crimson red. The rising sun brought a golden hue to the air with brilliant green punctuating through the ground fog.

The lake itself was dancing with clouds of fog with distant shorelines and docks coming in and out of view. At a distance, bumps on the calm water appeared and disappeared. A quick pull of the binoculars divulged the bumps to be two otters crossing from the east point of the bay to the west. Each dip under the water, lasting less than a minute, brought thoughts of what summer food the lake had provided them. Was it a population of crayfish this dry year?

In the late 1980's, many natural lakes of the Northwoods dropped 4 feet and the crayfish were abundant. With this drought, many aquatic plant species found in deeper waters disappeared, the rusty crayfish was blamed for this. No one connected that with less water in the lake, and the same amount of nutrients, the small free-floating plankton plants near the surface would absorb these nutrients and multiply prolifically. This in turn would shade and limit the growth of plants on the bottom. As soon as the water levels returned during wet years so did the vegetation on the lake bottom. I wonder if these otters live long enough to witness this eleven-year cycle of the Northwoods? This developed bay of Plum Lake always had crayfish and lots of submerged aquatic vegetation. The pair of otters soon reached the playground of an unoccupied dock on the west point.

My deliberation was broken by a large contingent of hooded merganser ducks paddling from the from east shoreline to west. Though standing motionless, I was quickly spotted by eighteen nearly grown ducklings with a thirty-six eyed security system that had kept them alive through the summer. On viewing me, they smoothly veered from the near shoreline into the wispy low fog and the now crimsoned light of the bay. The count was authenticated in open water as they seemed to form a receding chorus line materializing in and out of the fog. The otters had made a reverse trip now to a large dock area on the east point, where a third otter joined the ranks. The mother otter still had lessons for her brood to learn. The gaggle of ducks got a glimpse of this trio and systematically veered from this point. Again, the short time that these otters can hold their breath beneath the water in anticipation of a duck meal would be stymied by at least two of these thirty-six eyes. Or perhaps the otter at the same time, also knew the futility of any attempt and continued to play.

The silence of the early morning was interrupted suddenly by a lone boat steadily motoring from east to west. It returned a few minutes later in the opposite direction. On scoping the vessel, it appeared to be a game warden searching for one who might be disrupting nature in his eye or the law books. I hope he is appreciating this calm morning as it took four or five minutes for waves of his own disturbance to reach the shoreline at my feet ... it was time to go.

The morning chill settled into my stillness and I had to move on. As I did, an eagle now flew to the east point with a keen eye towards the merganser flock now three quarters across the calm lake. Maybe when the sun is higher, the shadows shorter, the wind rippling the lake surface, this flat lake dinner table will become a wrinkled tablecloth for its duck dinner. I found wild mint along the shoreline and placed it on the cabin's porch rail and knew the hot tea would warm my insides on return.

I walked north along the road through towering pines to stretch my stride. At the bend in the road a subtle change in the Northwoods was evident. An old bait shop that had been operated by a father and daughter at this boat landing for sixty years had been renovated to a small modern cabin and probably sold to someone with deep pockets without a true connection to the land. This scene seems a far distance in time from the bait shop's beginning when minnow and leach trapping and the resulting bait sales supported the family in summer and fish caught through the ice and deer venison of fall harvest fed the family in winter.

A less subtle change was a huge sign that warned fisherman that the Northwoods lakes were now threatened by eight different aquatic invasives and only <u>YOU</u> can do something about it. It reminded me of the Smokey the Bear campaign of the U.S. Forest Service that stopped fires but created a fear of fire to the demise of natural ecosystems. If man has moved across the landscape he has introduced intentionally, or not, new plants or animals; but now with too many people combined with too many land and water disturbances, this sign is just one more disruption of the wild. The story continues, but now it is written down and becomes a part of history whether we understand why, or not. Remember the rusty crayfish!

I quickly turn away through the valley where huge, tall white pines stretch my neck fully upward   to view their tops and determine the condition of their old age. Most continued to flourish with their bright soft green limbs evident in the clearness of dawn. As a field biologist I disdain the conservative label of any environmentalist as a "tree hugger", so I ironically wrapped my arms around a now dying white pine for another reason. My six-foot wingspan only reached a little over half of the circumference. This action was copied from a redneck logger, who determined a walnut was marketable if his reach could barely circumference the tree.

I am sure these virgin pines survived the logging of the Northwoods pinery over one hundred years ago as the origins of this old resort trumped the axe and crosscut saw of the lumberman. Once again, the aesthetics of the Northwoods prevailed over the progress. Yet, the silence of this once wilderness, just as the silence of this morning, will continue to be penetrated by the longer days of man's disturbances.

FALL

Autumn Chronicles

The fall of the year is a time for man to note what has happened throughout the growing season. The success or failures of the year are written in the colors, shapes, and patterns of the fall landscape. It is an opportunity to use the near silence of the season to rationalize what he has missed in the natural world.

It is not easy during the busy summer- or any time when the green foliage dominates the landscape - to associate where one plant begins and another ends. The tops of competing tree and shrubs intertwine, and it is hard to see the branches for the leaves- let alone which leaf belongs to which tree. The same questions can be ask of the closer shrubs and forbes in the undergrowth.

But when temperatures fall and clear sky gives you the tools to sort these things out, all becomes clear. Soon, the constant blur of green gives way to colors that separate the oak from the sugar maple, silver maple from the poplars, and apple from hazelnut. The colors do even more; the outline of each tree or shrub is now visible, the shape of a given specie is accented by a different color of the tree leaves behind it. Taller trees and individual branches are now visible to whisper to all who listen that this growing season has benefited me to survive and grow in the sea of summer green.

As one turns from forest to field the patterns and colors of fall are again evident in the competition between grasses and flowering plants. The abundance of the green growth of summer has now been painted by frost. Yellows, tans, browns, and even black now separate the quack from timothy, and the burdock from the milkweed on idle fields of abandoned farms. The tan-colored seed head of grasses dominate idle fields that have not been planted to the near evergreen alfalfa and clover of modern agriculture. If you are lucky to see a vanishing prairie, the pale reds are a stark contrast to the dull tan landscape of an abandoned field - this difference alone is another reason to plant a prairie and remind us what the natural world is all about.

If you slow down and look closer at the landscape of fall a subtle awareness of nature emerges. The presence of animals once hidden in the lush green foliage now become visible with the falling of leaves and the drooping of grasses. The repetitive paths of deer, fox, and mice moving from rest areas to the feeding areas of the growing season are threaded through the grassy scenery. Nests of squirrels and birds in shrubs and trees once hidden by the leaves of summer are suddenly silhouetted against the sky. New holes on the tree trunks and skeletal dead limbs now let us foresee that time is limited for all living things and that insects, birds, and squirrels are aware of when it is time for the living to move towards death graciously.

Finally, the colors and leaves succumb to rain, frost, and decay. One steadfast tree does not give into this process easily. The mighty oak has the last say 'pay attention to me, as I go, so does the land'. Indeed, the hardiest oak will become a sapling out of a deer's reach.

Eventually it will survive, flourish, and be a monument on the landscape in any season for many generations.

We need a parallel in the human species; Steadfast and mighty individuals who can lead civilization to understand the land ... and convince others that we can survive and flourish if we do.

September Mornings

When one awakes at the cabin in September you can find almost any occurrence of nature that signifies change and an end to a season. The growing season has intertwined and climbed like the Virginia Creeper vine, now reaching the heights of time that has sucked life from below and light from above and now clings to another being knowing the complexities of old age will soon end the cycle of life; but not before knowing it depends on other things for living.

The highest temperatures of August days now try to hold on but now give up to the fall coolness of night. This temperature changes spurs man to think of what will bring warmth in winter and he eyes what tree has ended its life but could continue its journey by giving flame to a fire. September stirs movement in man more than the heat of August.

Certainly, September wind knows no direction or temperature. A south wind that carried heat now carries a coolness. Birds now perch in areas protected from the south wind perceiving that this direction is where I should be heading soon. The north wind which once carried a coolness in summer now carries a cold that brings out gloves and caps. The ventures of the winds from the east and west are short-lived telling us changes will come quickly and that there are other points on the compass that are seldom visited the rest of the year. The wind shakes the leaves from their summer hold, bringing new vistas from the cabin porch. Open-framed views of the pond and valley below are now visible.

Growing green leaves releases life in a flutter of colors that eventually fail and fall to the ground. Summer leaf duties of bringing life and growth, can now be seen both hanging in a death silhouette and mixed or hidden on the good brown earth below. The annual cycle of nutrients is in full view.

The longer nights and shorter days change the sounds that reach anyone listening. Daytime bird songs of territories of the same species seem to be replaced by the communication between species. Maybe this is God's inventory saying " Yes, we can all exist in the same place if we understand each other". The daytime buzz of insects is delayed and limited by the now coolness that extends from dawn and quickly returns at dusk. This in return, modifies the main feeding periods for insect-feeding birds and at the same time cues them to thoughts of southernly flight.

Territories of other animals this time of year seem to expand for other reasons. There is plenty of food for many species higher in the food chain; Fruits of ground plants and trees are now abundant for squirrels, deer, raccoons, and bears. Yet the habitats that contain these foods seem to only dot our modern landscape and corridors connecting the dots are scarce. Movement of our largest mammals in fall correspond to an urge to reproduce and feed for the long winter ahead, but without safe corridors between dots there is an irony; human corridors of roads lead to their demise - not survival.

Maybe the chills of September have a purpose. We close the windows and doors of our home and at the same time shut out the sounds of nature we have enjoyed all summer. As the day warms, we might open these frames to the natural world for a few hours to hear this diminished sound from nature. Could this same shelter we so cherish all year during this instance in September give us a clue to a future of the fading life around us if we do not start paying attention to it more closely.

Part 2: OUT OF STEP

Passing of the Land

How soon will the land say enough? How soon will the land say too much? What will it take before the weight of human culture will no longer be endured by the land and its ability to adjust to its desecration? These are questions that should be asked now, not when pessimism looms in the shadows and the sun is about to set.

There are ecological problems in our world that are so extensive and identification so remote to our everyday lives that they tend to be ignored by most and debated by those who need to act. Over thirty years ago many of these large problems were recognized. Over population, ozone depletion & air pollution, water shortages, energy consumption, water pollution, and world food provision were only a few problems that would have to be solved by thinking man. Our answer for most was that technology would find the answer.

Birth control, sterilization, and the technology of warfare would take care of the overpopulation. Yet man's sociobiological rendering to himself does everything to make sure his genetic code survives; If I am to lose children through famine and starvation, I must produce more children in hope that at least one survives. Those who try to meet the problem head on are met with other moralistic factions that say life must go on for all humans and make personal decisions for others. Warfare kills people and the destruction of the land is collateral damage. Yet the rest of the members of the plant and animal kingdom live and die in the shadows of our human habitation.

Ozone depletion and air pollution appears a truly remote problem as we cannot see it and our ancestors have always viewed the sky as separated from the land. It is ironic that these problems of the air we breathe locally appear to be the collective space where all the problems on the land accumulate and the now affect all areas that are remote from their origin. What appears even more incredulous to us is that it can descend again in our backyard or effect what we thought was a wilderness undisturbed by man. The lines drawn in the sand over this form of sky degradation must be erased. The remoteness and vast effects it has on the earth are an overwhelming wave that erases the line before it is clearly identified. If there is a type of earth degradation that is reflective of the mass societies we have created, this one is the one that will keep us from seeing the setting sun.

Water shortages were first recognized over forty years ago in the Southwest of the United States, where the concentration of people was faced with nature providing a limited amount of rain. At that time technology was going to fix the problem by building a dual-purpose desalting plant off the coast that would produce fresh water and electricity by heat distillation. They also looked to reverse osmosis filtering and cloud seeding to dump more water into the Colorado River. Today they are still looking for more water and other areas of the arid southwest have populated to a point where there is no more water available. Today large pipelines are being built to transfer oil products; how soon will they be used to transfer water?

When will man learns to live within his means and adapt to his environment rather than taking this destructive route? Will we see the setting sun by removing the clouds? Do we always need to be doing something that requires power? Power plants are a necessity to provide electricity for computers, washer & dryers, heaters & air conditioners, and televisions. Fuel is a requirement for automobiles, tractors, generators, construction equipment, home heating equipment, all-terrain vehicles, power boats, and snowmobiles. We look to technology to produce more energy with less pollution. We looked to technology to create machines that use less energy. These energy consuming machines originally were tools to make necessary work easier and faster, therefore creating more free time. Yet the creation of these machines has carried over to the toys of our free time and distorted our perspective of recreation. Today, do we take this extra time to understand what are the real necessities or what the basic requirements are for a healthy life? If we do this, we will find it is the simple life with less power that makes us healthy and happy. The real setting sun can be viewed from a hilltop that we have walked up.

Water is not just two parts hydrogen and one-part oxygen. It is a medium that supports all life on earth. We have done our best to foul it in the form of acid rain, ground water pollution, and in the disturbances of aquatic habitats. Our lakes and streams were once convenient direct dumping grounds for human, lumber mill, and paper production waste, and a variety of what we thought harmless chemical compounds. If there was not a lake or stream nearby the nearest low-lying area or wetland was the next most convenient site.

With industrial development came expanded use of boilers that could burn waste of an industry or any fuel available sending the waste into the atmosphere. Technology, with advances in chemistry and gas chromatography, was quick to recognize these contaminations into the atmosphere.

We have also created a regime of pollution laws to attempt to stop any further degradation from occurring. We have created some funds and a few methods for cleanup, but in most cases these remedial solutions are outrageously expensive and only store waste from further exposure to humans in the future. With this comes protection of the site from human health but extensions of risk management to another living organism is not a priority. Worse yet, we have prevailed in taking polluted site technology to create economic opportunities for redevelopment of the site what we call a government guarantee of Certification of Completion. Yet with all this effort, what mechanism have we developed to ensure that future decisions regarding the land, whether political or economic, are made with the health of the land first in both heart and soul? Setting suns come with reflections of our past lives.

Where will our next meal come from? It is protein we need to grow. Thirty years ago, we looked to our vast world oceans as the solution for this need for protein. The advent the technology of satellite imagery and radar to track and discover vast schools of fish to feed the world, we have observed instead collapses of our fisheries and vast plumes and deltas of polluted soil and human waste entering from the land. Science has documented these large deltas and plumes have exceeded the natural process of nutrients returning to the sea and being recycling into the ocean's fishery. These soils were from the exposed lands of agriculture and progress that was attempting to feed the world from the land. The degraded makeup of the silt in the delta of rivers has either prevented the food chain recycling process from occurring or made the recycling product as fish and seafood unsafe to eat because of the chemical pollutants.

How many children will be here to see a final sunset? How many children will be starve and die before this darkness occurs?

An Accumulation of Knowledge

We have been gaining knowledge for a long time. Knowledge that has created inventions so we could store it. From papaya scrolls to the books of Gutenberg's printing press, to the computer. We now have collected so much knowledge that we have come up with search engines that put it at our fingertips. Yet have we advanced, as humans, to use this knowledge wisely?

Just as an old professor told me in his retirement, most people do not reach a level of understanding that is called wisdom until they reach the age sixty... and many never will develop thought into wisdom at all. Extending this adage to humans and our use of knowledge to take care of the earth, one is not sure we are developing any wisdom and the possibility we never will.

A few wise people of this planet, that are and were true thinkers with wisdom, have come up with the field of ecology that places things on this biosphere in a connected lot. They realize the importance of these connections and their intricate webbings by reaching out to understand them even further as they know life on earth depends on them. Others who reach for the wisdom and understanding of this ecological paradigm shift are modeling these webs and their interactions or inventorying the species that make up the web. Yet are we applying this knowledge in time to preserve the webs that sustain us ... realizing man as only a small part of the dynamic evolving system of life?

We do things for the benefit of man not for all living things. We do not yet realize that the quality of our life on earth dependents on the health of other living organisms. We must realize as with other animals, when we become too abundant the land that supports us is no longer capable of doing so. Humans have been intelligent in devising a way to survive and prosper, but eventually the plight of man is the same as all forms of life — too big of a population with not enough resources to support them.

Will there comes a time when man sees his place in nature as a creature among other creatures; not as a predator that can destroy both species and the habitat that supports all life. Natural disasters caused by man, such as massive oil spills, are examples how greed trumps wisdom. Mankind obsession to need more and more possessions to advance their standard of living is not the answer to man's purpose. When will the basics of life be enough for man once again? Ethics is an extension of wisdom and a wise man, Aldo Leopold, once said " Something is right when it preserves the ecological integrity, aesthetics, and is economically expedient, to do otherwise it is not".

Common Ground

There are patterns that are common in all the world that we now recognize but barely visualize their importance. These patterns are woven intricately in nature and unraveled unknowingly by man's nature. They occur in nature from one continent to another, from one country to another, and have no borders that we should recognize. These common patterns go from one ecosystem to the next. Decades of research for the understanding the importance of connections between ecosystems will come too late. We must recognize the common ground now.

Disturbances in plant communities and loss of predator and large animal populations appear to be causing catastrophic changes in ecosystems. Both disturbances are prompted by the need to promote an agricultural economy and to feed an ever-increasing population of humans. But if you look at the long-term picture of the results we are in a pattern of diminishing returns.

In the long run the diets and environment that we have created out of these needs for meat and grains have diminished the health of the human population. Major cancers today are being linked to diets and exposure to carcinogenic chemicals that came with the agricultural revolution that destroyed the prairies. Medical understanding of these pathogens will soon lead us to explanations, but to understand the path of destruction of an ecosystem that got us here will go without much notice until we recognize we now need a soil for sustenance we no longer have or can easily recreate.

Diseases and ecosystem destruction patterns are evident in all our disturbed ecosystems if we can reach beyond our anthropomorphic values and recognize them. Over population of any species profoundly affects other species on all trophic levels. Examples from rabies to distemper in canine populations to fungus diseases that wiped out populations of American chestnut and elms in the eastern forest: there are thousands of similar occurrences throughout the world that are attributed to human disruptions of natural life cycles.

The snowballing disturbances of diseases throughout the planet because of man's actions can now be traced back to the loss of top predators and habitat loss due increased human populations. Disease, natural food chain collapse, and loss of predator-prey relationships will continue to increase as we move more towards a world economy with the movement of products to feed and meet the "expected" cultural expectations of the world population.

For decades we have trumpeted that the water that covers most of this planet will produce the protein needed for our exponential growth in world population. Where removal of predators on the land have caused drastic changes in the landscape, we have chosen not to replace them in most cases because we believe we can assume that role. Beneath the water we have had a different approach.

Through overfishing we have overexploited and eliminated both predator and prey species. Often in their place we have chosen to stock only predator species, and often an exotic, to meet false expectations of catch and harvest.

On the land and sea other exotics now move into an ecosystem filling the void left by the depleted species or capitalizing on the declining habitat that remains. The biological production and potential harvest from that ecosystem decreases with every change in specie from those that originally inhabited the ecosystem. These actions are occurring in our aquatic systems from the smallest ponds to our largest lakes, to the productive shoals of our ocean shorelines to the open ocean. What resources of the future are we going to turn to feed us?

Discover the Connection!

Where will we find the way to link all the people of this planet to the notion that all life is dependent upon a cooperation of each part? We as "thinking beings" can create ideals to live for the good of the human individual and societies but why have we not done the same for all life on this planet?

There are certain personified species and individuals who have lived among nature that folk lore and Hollywood have brought to our attention. Will we in time develop an ecological consciousness that can find faith in the facts that lie hidden in these fabled lessons that can be brought to light in the plight of the earth's resources tomorrow?

Romulus and Remus, two fabled human sons of Roman culture, were raised and protected by wolves. We now know that wolf culture is genetically and instinctively set for the survival of the young of the dominate reproducing individuals in the pack family, which the entire family takes part in the raising of the young. Today it is a model of what the human family needs in these hard times of individualism and perceived independence.

We instead continue to see the wolf as a too effective predator of deer that competes with the recreational hunter. With villainous passion we continue to demonize the wolf of the fairy tales of *Little Red Riding Hood* and the *Three Little Pigs* and extend these misplaced feelings into efforts to stymie their ecological role. If we look further into the knowledge, we have gathered about the ecology of the wolf we will find they are also predators of mice and other rodents that are even more abundant on our landscape. As part of our environmentally aware culture this one creature symbolizes the passion of life and the compassion of relationships. Modern human culture seems to be losing this care and compassion.

In the 1950's and 60's the silver screen of Hollywood projected scenes from the wilderness jungles in their *Tarzan* sequels. It is here where a man lived among the animals of a jungle and understood the interactions and relationship of all creatures who lived there. As part of each sequel there was interaction of civilized men seeking adventure, wealth, or knowledge of a place where man and his environment were in harmony. The actions of civilized man were represented by anthropologist, news seeking reporters, big game hunters, and those who sought the riches of past civilizations. Tarzan represented man in nature not above it. He understood it as a way of life, tried to make his fellow man grasp its meaning, and protected it with the help of his fellow creatures who were part of the jungle. In the end a civilized person named Jane came to understand and love the interactions and simplicities of the jungle life, returned, and became part of it. This depiction of wilderness also gave America a sense of living in the natural state during a time when rapid agriculture cultivation and domestic materialism overtook our cultural thinking. The movies were again an escape from reality of a society but toted a lesson or two as Hollywood always has.

Today we continue to exploit the jungle we now know as rain forest. We continue to destroy hunter and gatherer cultures in the guise of social and economic development while knowing what we are doing is not morally right. We do not fully recognize and embrace our own ethical failing culture. We have not yet used our knowledge of life on this planet to extend our passions to preserving the threads of nature that makes all life possible to all. Man can correct these actions and inaction's - it is in his genetic being and soul to do so.

What is Right?

There are as many reasons to do things right as there are to do things wrong. There are habits that keep us from doing either. Regarding the land and our environment, we are doing a lot of wrong things. The habits of modern culture proliferate the wrong actions that negatively affect our land and prevent humans moving forward to save ourselves.

It appears environmental awareness has made great strides, yet the destruction of the earth continues as our populations and economies consume more and more of it. Is there a perspective that can help us change our ways? Man is the "thinking being" and his intellectual advancement over millions of years is because of his ability to adapt to the environment he has been faced with. We are now faced with the dilemma of atmospheric destruction so severe it may end life on earth. Can we do what is right and change our ways or are we doomed by our habits?

79

I believe the answer to our dilemma – just as most answers- is looking at the past. The hunter and gatherer cultures have lasted for many more millennium than our agricultural modern society without destroying their world. Should we be asking those hunter gather societies that remain what they do when faced with a death situation? Do they react today as if there was no tomorrow? Do they not worry about tomorrow as they are in the hands of a God who provides for today and tomorrow? Did they use the simple tools and methods available to them to survive? There is nothing simple about the way we live today, and they had the same thoughts about their culture.

Where cultivation and civilizations destroyed the native plant and animal communities of an area, hunter and gatherer societies soon disappeared. When these new culture and modern ideas of how to produce food for the masses made life easier for them, soon the ways that once sustained them before were forgotten. Are these ancient forgotten lessons being repeated in our modern culture? To this end we are still destroying the land that sustains us today on an even bigger scale called Planet Earth.

Is it not logical to look at agriculture in a form where it does not consume the land and continue to destroy natural habitat? Organic farming and rotational grazing are a start to a process that may lead to sustainable agriculture. The next step is to move towards restoration of native plant communities in the grasslands of grazers and choose crop species that maintain the integrity of soil and have attributes of natural pest control. The cost of large equipment, seed, and fertilizer to produce a product on the soil of the land that is heavily subsidized and then over processed to a point where it is nutritionally faulted is not a scenario that sustains humans or the planets life support systems.

The adage that "time repeats itself" is always true with a twist. Things have gone global with the economy and environmental destruction, it can again go local when things need to be righted, again. Our ability to reason what is necessary for survival is found in the human genetic code and modernization that destroys a culture is not.

Evolution

I remember my grandfather's collection of National Geographic Society publications that included even the earliest additions. My ancestors were Swedish immigrants that migrated through Latvia to America. I suspect they knew that humans had a lot to see and observe in this world and their survival was dependent on understanding the world; Any place they were to call home and at a higher perspective brought to them by their long association with the magazine.

Reading an old December 1971 issue of the National Geographic one can only except our existence and place on earth, as my grandfather saw it, as a fascinating place brought to them in photos and words. One wonders if all of mankind was able to read, view, and understand how the earth's species and communities exist and evolve, without man's influences but despite his influences, humans would make better decisions to sustain all life.

This Geographic issue highlighted the characteristics of the shy, highly intelligent, but misunderstood world of the octopus. Here is an animal, just as people now inhabited much of the terra firma of the world, has lived, and evolved in every corner of the world's oceans. This marvelous creature faces the pressures of man's expanded existence because, as ugly we perceive it, it tastes good to today's fastest expanding human populations.

A third article of this issue introduced the rest of the world to the emerging and changing Chinese culture that at that time was on the verge of entering the modern world of industry and commerce. This change is now occurring with a hope for an increased standard of living of the world's largest population that will test the ability of this planet to sustain us.

Another short essay described a newly discovered culture of hunter and gatherers, the Tasada tribe, found in the forests of the southern Philippines. After a neighboring tribe's trapper discovered them on the edge of his domain and gave them tools that made their lives easier this small self-sustaining community still chose to use their traditional tools. Did they know in their subconscious that these tools might represent changes in their lives that meant the end of their culture.... a change, though it made life simpler, would eventually lead to a more complex life? If we look at today's society in the developed world, how many of our woes are tied to new tools and this complex life?

Aboriginal cultures, our past civilizations, and intelligent creatures of the sea and land have a lot to teach us about what is important for our future survival and evolution. I hope the National Geographic will continue to reach the world of modern man so he can proceed with a reasoning of his place in this world, be humbled by it, and limit his actions for its continuance.

In Our Own Back Yard

The loss of diversity in nature is coupled with patterns left by progress. We build roads and create development that changes the everyday path that living organisms have traveled throughout time. An example is that we disturb or destroy plant communities that are intricately woven in sustaining mammal populations of both predator and prey. The wolf, coyote, and fox predator populations depend on the deer, rabbit, and mouse populations, that in return are based on the plant species in their habitat.

These predator and prey animals are mobile as humans. As an example, they can carry plant seeds or pathogens, equally well throughout their daily and seasonally routines as well as through the plant communities in which they live. These seeds and pathogens are often exotics from another continent. As a creature of habit, animals in their mobility of hunting and feeding will carry these foreign organisms throughout their range until they become well established.

We try to make decisions to stop the spread: destroy or stop human transport or transmittal; eliminate or reduce the organism that covey them; and put great efforts to study cause and effect. Little effort is placed on diversity restoration and conservation. These diversity actions are best in the defense of exotic organisms. Choosing and restoring pre-settlement native plants and their communities is a must for success where diversity has been lost.

Plant choices for restoration should include pre-settlement vegetation and maintaining soil integrity. To take the sun's energy and create a complex earth biosphere is a saga based on our dear plants. The lush green of a springtime morning awes the eye with life. The deer browsing the plant life to support the fawn within is the unseen miracle.

The act of the deer foraging brings insects aloft as the phoebe snaps it up in its beak and then returns it to the nest brood of yawning young. The deer chooses its browsed plants carefully- the exotic garlic mustard plant is ignored. But seeds of this mustard plant clings to the deer, eventually falls off, and seeds other areas that create plants ,that in turn compete with the plants that sustain the deer. Those native plants that sustain other animals in the web of life needs our help through ecological restoration now.

We will never be able to fully understand the intricacies of ecology, but we can assume that all things are connected physically, chemically, and biologically. We must assume all parts are important and be in a position today to identify the parts that are missing and put them back. That is restoration at it is simplest. Make sure the parts are there, again. Make sure that these parts are in place so the functioning of plant communities and ecosystems can start again. Your own back yard is the place to start!

Land Time

America is a nation of vast terrains with a diversity of natural resources that have provided us wealth and power. We have developed diverse government and private conservation organizations to protect other resources as we withdraw from beneath and upon the land. Why is it then that the path that we are following is creating a vengeful terrain? There is something wrong with the system. Can we fix it?

Our attitude towards the land is that the products that come from it will never be exhausted and that we will always have alternatives to its consumption. Yet the alternatives we have chosen in the long run are just as consumptive.

In rural America prior to the 1940s wood products were used for construction, heating, and cooking. A good deal of life revolved around cutting wood from the forest. Man's spirit, exercise, food, and shelter all revolved around being on the land. It was hard work but a good life.

The radio was only the second to the wood burner as the main piece of furniture in the living room. One day the radio announced that at the rate that we were depleting our forest, we would run out of wood in a short time. Rural America believed this message and changed its ways. They accepted fuel oil and electricity. What they did not realize, but excepted, was resource of energy that was not local and costly; but was a beginning to a better, and easier life.

The same rural farmer produced his food from the open land next to the forest or woods. The animals and plants of the farm, both wild and domestic, provided a surplus beyond the family needs. The waste from the animals and garden was returned to the land. The land was happy to receive it, producing more crops and animal products the next year. Any extra production was given or bartered to neighbors. Further excess was sold to others in the nearby communities to provide food, heat, and build shelter. In return money for products sold purchased items for their extra needs and simple luxuries. These were purchased with saved money on the few trips to town each year.

But with electricity in the barn the new radio told the farmer that the urban population was growing, and that the farmer must produce more to feed them. Besides this, there was little land available for our sons and daughters to get their own farm started so they moved to town to work at the creamery, mill, or main street store.

Now the removal from the land was to accelerate. The family was not just over the hill from grandma's house. To make wood for heat and cooking without family help was too much and that oil burner did not sound like a bad idea. The squirrels one ate for dinner once a week, because junior could provide them with few short enjoyable hours in the forest were no longer harvested. He was working long hours at the milk and cheese creamery in town or on the next ridge. The better life was on its way.

The products that once came to and from the local community by train now traveled greater distances by truck. We needed the motor vehicles to go farther and faster ... and, of course, the road had to be smooth for us to enjoy the ride. The burden to tax the land to build the roads would be added to the pressures on the land for food production. The fact that the road building and the driving of motor vehicles would over time destroy the air we breathe and the segments of the land we love and needed did not matter.

Now we move to the big city to build cars. We accumulate wealth and now want to go back to the land to spend it. We buy fancy bicycles, snowmobiles, ATVs, and horses to ride. We buy boats, fancy canoes, and personal watercraft to float. We need a place to ride and float. So, we need to develop the old railway right-a-ways and build more river and lake accesses. If these accesses are not out our own back door, we need better roads to get there faster because we need recreation to relax from the everyday fast pace. Is there something wrong with the better life?

Humans and Their Land

Forty years ago, when discussing the directions that land conservation was headed, the main question was actions are going to save the natural world from mankind, laws or education? What should have been asked was how long would it take man's political processes, I short-sightedness, self-importance, and greed to bring about the demise of his own kind. This is a tale of the life and death of a small farm community in hope for a wise man to change direction and do what is right.

In the beginning there was this mile-high glacier slowly moving about its business of crushing rock into finer materials that eventually became soil. Depending on where the glacier went, or how long it lingered in one spot, what it pushed in front of it, and what got carried with the melting flow from it, the soil and rock ended up in different sizes at different elevations and locations.

Add a little heat, and goodbye glacier, hello landforms and natural landscapes. Water flowed out from beneath the glacier or was left large ice blocks that slowly melted over hundreds of years because of the soil that had buried it insulated it. A terrible physical modern example of this would be when snow is pushed off your drive into an area of your yard and the sod of your lawn covers some of the snow. What snow is the last to melt in your yard each spring?

On the bigger landscape, depending on the size of the ice chunk and the depression it made, a big lake, a pothole pond, or just a lowly wetland slowly evolved. For tens of thousands of years all three were essential to other aquatic and semi aquatic creatures, or palatable food ... think wild rice or even a cattail root, or even as habitat where a deer or moose could be hiding.

But the land higher on the landscape than the lake, pond, and wetland was to become more important as civilizations developed and humans got lazy. It was easier to enslave others, lead a horse or oxen, and eventually drive a tractor than stalk wildlife so he became a farmer or urban dweller. Man could now live in the city as the farmer could bring food to him. Besides, he thought the critters would like the free food he now provided as a farmer. He thought he was a conservationist now and all the wildlife needed was his crops .

The farmer bought more tractors and gadgets to farm more land. On dry years he was able to farm a little more of the wetland but on other wet years he could not, but still wanted the production to pay the increased taxes and cost of seed that was always increasing. So, drain tile was invented. Then came bigger equipment to plant and harvest crops quicker because nature did not always cooperate. He justified getting rid of the fence rows separating pastures and woodlands to increase the yield and lost production of wet "wetland" years. Also, that bigger equipment mirrors were being tore off when trying to get an extra row of crop on the field edge. There go the fence rows, forest ... and more wildlife habitat.

Even with agricultural tax breaks and subsidies on crops it was more profitable for agribusinessmen to bulldoze woodlands and make it into cropland. Long term return on forest products and wildlife habitat was not enough. Industrial agriculture was born.

Now the grasses, forbes, shrubs, and trees in the fence rows, wetlands and woodlands that supported all wildlife with food and cover are gone. Minor crop pest, that had competition or were once preyed on by wildlife, now flourished. The farmer's expenses increased further in the form of pesticides, and genetically altered seed to solve the pest problem. In addition, the cover or habitat for larger mammals and birds that were used for travel from one wetland or woods to another are no longer there. Their home for reproduction and a variety of food that they need for survival are gone or reduced to small places. The game species, bird species, and insects that once formed the food chains of nature are reduced or eliminated. The farmer says more fertilizer, genetics, pesticides, ... and yes, more farmland are needed so I can feed the world. The farmer says, "I need to farm more acres to make things work" and the follows with " things aren't as they used to be, and I can't figure out why"?

Good hunting land is now a commodity for the rich as there is few good habitats remaining and the hunter can thank the farmer ... and let us not forget the developer who can make more profitable use of the expensive farmland. The conservationist is now a tree hugger with no land but public land to protect and use, but often being a hunter, must try to separate himself from tree hugger.

What we humans do not realize, and seldom admit, we too are animals that need habitat and the environment. We have become global. Our farm field is now the Planet Earth.

Man's Earthly Decline

There will be a time when man will no longer controls this Planet Earth. It will come after the ills of greed have decimated nature; and nature will fight back in ways not imagined or predicted. It is already happening.

The large mammals that are omnivores have reacted already. The American black bear whose population is growing utilizing human waste and excess. Human food waste, bird and corn feeding for wildlife feeding, can carry them through the bleak times when nature does not provide their needs. Recreational home construction that opens canopy of forest to more light increases successional shrubbery and wild berry production ... also increase bear food sources.

White-tailed deer populations continue to increase in most areas especially in areas lacking heavy snowfall and forest cover. Crops, successional shrub browse, misaligned political population control by man now have created a phenomenal food source for two top carnivorous predators: the mountain lion, and the wolf. In Wisconsin both are expanding their ranges from northern Wisconsin into southern Wisconsin.

A wolf monitoring and management program falters with protected and unprotected status as the population continues to grow. Telemetry provides a look at this growth, yet the pack status can change abruptly as the population grows and the unmarked individuals are soon lost in the statistics of technology and government conservation budgets. If the deer population continues to expand, so will the wolf population. The wolf is a more effective predator of deer than man. Man, in his laziness will eventually not be able contribute to land health through the cropping of deer through game laws and management. Man reacts by wanting to shoot the wolf... not understanding or caring that the wolf is a better predator and land manager.

The mountain lion is one of the most effective predators we will ever encounter. Their nocturnal habits and stealth approach to predation enables them to increase on a land abundant in deer without much notice. Instinctively, predators are opportunists.

Fenced and corralled livestock and domestic species in their territories can become easy prey. Humans are not beyond their reach as pre , yet the presence of man in the silent and night woods are not very often encountered in America.

Beyond these trends of large mammal population increases we ponder on the reason why our telltale medium-size mammal, the coyote, is ever on the increase in areas where marginal or no habitat is found. The coyote has never been subject to the laws of man but are keen to take advantage of his unknown detrimental effects on the land. The old American Indian adage "When all living things on earth perish, the song dog will prevail". This proverb has teeth that will not let go of history. The sound of the wild on the domesticated landscape will always have the howl of the coyotes at night. Again, their efficiencies at survival and expansion on mice, rabbit, deer, or any scrap carrion waste of man's interference with nature is a sign that there is something wrong with the way man abuses it.

Micro Ecology

Today's world is full of the scientific inquiry of the microcosm. Yearly, technology unfolds more knowledge of storage microchips, genetic engineering, viral plagues, and bacterial diseases. We are even creating a microscopic world to the extent that we can take the combined knowledge of each field and make solid physical structures. What nano culture will find the natural world important? What effort are we making to understand how the microworld connects to the natural macrocosm that we barely contemplate now?

In the biology of aquatic systems, we have identified in our microscopic world single-celled plants we call algae. Some are called green algae that are at the base of the aquatic food chain. We often call them phytoplankton and they are eaten by zooplankton, forage fish, amphibians, and invertebrates - which in turn are eaten by larger fish, larger invertebrates and mammals.

A second algae we named blue green algae appeared to have a different role in the natural world. Few animals were able to consume it and many types are highly toxic to humans, livestock, and other animals. The presence of low numbers of blue green algae is common in healthy ecosystems as they are much like a storage bin of nutrients waiting for the right time to become part of the food chain. Yet, the last thousand years with the industrial ability to expose and move large volumes of erodible earth and to impound water the blue green algae have flourished. With their abundance has come problems that brought more study of it. We in fact have renamed it cyanobacteria.

Single cell algae have been touted as one of the first photosynthesizing organisms on earth and that all living forms of organic life started with it. It is likely that blue green algae or cyanobacteria was the first pre-plant to live in a volcanic world of toxins, storing nutrients until the mutations of time could diversify and utilize them as primitive plants. As always time repeats itself - the storage of nutrients and toxins has gone full circle. But evolution and time has created a creature with the ability to reason that separates it from the rest of the world. Why cannot humanity reason that this proliferation of this primeval microorganism is telling us that we are losing diversity? Small hints of mammals and waterfowl being poisoned are not enough.

Nature has developed a way to resist disturbances caused by both natural phenomena and man. We have created a science called ecology to understand the interactions of organisms with their environment, but when are we going to advance that science to recognize the checks and balances of nature and elevate man's thinking to a level to save himself? We have just dawned on the information age. The computer can store information that our cluttered brain only dreams of. But who is to feed a computer with all the facts of an ecosystem? Who is to create a program that can follow the ever-changing dynamics of a living organisms or recognize that that life is in trouble – before this natural program is about to crash?

Our Deer Society

The white-tailed deer population in Wisconsin may be reaching an all-time high. Our recorded deer population history only extends back to the 1950s, but we have empirical history the population could have been just as high in the late 1930s through the 1940s. At that time, the deer population exploded with the abundance of second growth vegetation after the clearcutting of the hardwoods and pines prior. When this second growth got out of reach and the human population began to harvest the reproductive females the population declined. But at present, the herd continues to expand without the human capacity to control their numbers. Are we are wrong to manage it as a crop?

The reasons for this uncontrolled population expansion and the solution to it comes from many angles each with their own justification and prejudices. Some game biologists' reason that our social traditions of shooting a buck is the main cause in our inability to control the herd. They contend if we target does first, we may be able to reduce the herd by reducing their reproductive capacity. But, in the long run this social tradition and the camaraderie of the hunt is what keeps the hunter a field generation after generation. If it easy to shoot a deer because they are so plentiful, or if the deer population declines, will the challenge of nature still be there to hold the interest of future generations?

Our booming economy and lifestyles appear to have lifted our sustenance from the land which further erodes our hunting tradition. Yet time and culture allow for gaps and losses of tradition; stories, books, and now videos cannot replace actual experiences.

Our modern culture is now moving towards a diet away from the industrial agricultural enterprises that produce beef, pork, and lamb that so changed the landscape. Could this change in culture lead us back to the land to reduce the deer herd? Venison is a healthy protein source and very plentiful in the agricultural areas of Wisconsin. The demand for production of grain crops and legumes for beef and swine is decreasing but the demand for them to feed the dairy cow and the winter feeding of deer is increasing.

The missing links in making deer a commodity is the control of supply and demand. The white-tailed deer is a wild animal governed by possession limits and seasons of take. Over the last 20 years, as the deer population has increased, our take has increased due to quota changes in possession limits and increased pressures to bring the herd size down. The bow, gun, and traditional muzzle loader hunters have lengthened the traditional deer gun season in the name of gaining a quality hunt for each of their peers. The game biologist regulators have increased bag potentials through an increase in doe harvest permits to reduce the reproductive potential. Neither seem to have worked to reduce the deer population when needed for sustained periods. There are continuing efforts to extend the season further to further increase deer harvest.

But our traditions of harvest and seasons are still held firm. The quality of the hunt is often expressed in the number of deer that are viewed. The avid trophy hunter now passes up dozens of deer to take a large rack that has now gained a monetary value that exemplifies the mass commercialization of the sport. But the fact that the deer over-abundance that alters habitat and survival of other species is not commonly recognized. Man has created conditions ideal for the whitetail but is unable to resolve problems associated with their overabundance. He is still anthropomorphic in the handling of this problem in that he alone is affected, and he can reduce the herd. Wildlife biologists familiar with ecological principles know that other predators are needed to bring the situation under control but will not openly support it considering the still more steadfast and old traditions against predators.

But Wisconsin can boast of one of the best deer management programs in the nation! Will it take an epizoic calamity of CWD (Chronic Wasting Disease) expansion or another mammal (this includes humans) catastrophic illness to change society attitudes? Or can our increased knowledge of nature and humble our egos to realize we aware that we are part of the land - not above the land as a creator or destroyer.

Patterns

There are many survival characteristics of other animals that humans have lost, but our gain in our ability to reason should compensate these losses.   From the compound eye of the insect to the human-like eyes of mammals the ability to pick out patterns in nature are a key to all animal survival. Human ability to pick out patterns is a key to our survival- but we need to do it soon and react quicker than our ancestors.

The eye of the insect can align objects they have discovered to the position and angle of the sun.   When a single scout honeybee or ant discovers a new food source, it is this navigational trait that leads other workers to a food source or another colony. It is the study of insects that have led to many discoveries of how ecosystems function, interact, survive, and successfully thrive. These are the lessons that humans must adapt to as populations grows to superior organism status.

Have you ever tried to sneak up on a deer? With no wind- or working up wind- it is possible. If you try it standing up it is impossible no matter how slow you move. For what a deer sees at a distance is not you but a shape or form out of focus that represents an object that was not there a minute ago. A movement will distinguish and define the shape as a man. Color- especially white can set off the alarm response signaled by its own white flag as it heads in the other direction. Specific patterns in clothing also can bring quicker attention as the camouflaged individual knows. If you get on your hands and knees with grasses as cover and breaking up your pattern, sneaking up on a deer becomes easier. As you get closer a deer will often snort … clearing its nose as if its own nose has deceived it by not recognizing your smell and needs a good cleaning out. And then it stomps the ground in attempt to scare you into the movement that separates prey and predator. If you cannot come into focus and you continue to approach slowly it will flee.

Have you ever watched a deer flee at a dead run across an open field or a steep ravine? In the steep ravine there is only one rock that the deer must land on and launch from to cross the ravine. It can identify it at a full speed. In an open field, if startled, it travels hundreds of yards at a dead run in a straight line and enters a single well used runway that leads off the field into the wetland and woods for cover and safety. If you look closely there is usually a large tree or a large rock with a very distinguishing canopy or silhouette that the deer has retained in its memory that has honed him into the safety runway he has used before. We then must wonder where the phrase "Dead Run" must come from as it is an instinct for living not dying.

What patterns are we to see? We are beginning to recognize patterns of disturbances we have caused, but as with the deer we are trying to recognize something in the distance ...that is out of focus. Man's reasoning can identify the results of these disturbances ... like a loss of species. For an example, we now know that depletion in freshwater fisheries may not be caused by over exploitation alone but also by the loss of aquatic vegetation and habitat. The missing birds from the backyard of Wisconsin are from loss of plant species habitat from here to Brazil.

In our modernized society, that has little connection to the land, we expect that these patterns of disturbance can be fixed by government conservation. What we do not realize is that these disruptions have occurred over decades and centuries. What we see are the results of cumulative problems associated with natural resource use and depletion. In over one hundred years of government conservation the true patterns of species loss continue. We have failed to convey the message to those on the land, and those removed from the land, that our continued conservation actions that do not address the broader solutions of economy will not ensure our survival. Our traveling down this same path without taking the fragmented patterns and putting them back together will continue to destroy what was once sustainable.

Our government conservation has turned to technology in solving our problems of air pollution, human and animal waste, and resource consumption. But what gains have we made in our patterns of land protection. We are just forming methods of recognizing land use and abuses, then spending millions of dollars on purchasing land without gains in ecological land protection and restoration.

How long will it be before land stewardship becomes common sense? Will it be before, as stated in 1992 by the Union of Concerned Scientists World Warning to Humanity, "Vast human misery is to be avoided and our global home on this planet is not to be irretrievably mutilated."?

Short Grass

There is an iconic symbol of our present society that stands out to warn us of what is to come- short grass. Its presence for any length of time has always been associated with man's disturbance of what was once was sustainable and wild. It is the progression of the wild to the domestic to the loss of sustainability.

The first image of the problem with short grass came to play in the beginning of civilization over 7,000 years ago in the mountains separating Persia from Mesopotamia. Shepherds of goats and sheep tried to supply the population of Mesopotamia that has been estimated at the time between 17 and 25 million. Deforestation followed by heavy grazing led to erosion that in return lead to the siltation of the rivers and canals used for irrigation. A fertile valley remains today but in an arid land without irrigation and without 'mountain forest humidity to bring rain to the area, it has not recovered. One ponders that at the end of their civilization, when the confusion of tongues at the tower of Babel occurred, the word 'conservation' was not in their vocabulary. This same scenario spread across the continents over time to be repeated in China, Africa, Europe, and the Americas. Where lies the omen of short grass when sterile stony ground and wasting gullies become the landscape?

Grasses at one time covered over one third of the earth. The relationship between modern agriculture and grazing has personified the short grass. The fruit of the grass is the grain that feeds both the wild and the domestic including us- the latter because it can be dried, easily stored and transported. The grass leaf cannot be eaten by humans but can be converted to protein in the form of red meat and milk by cows, deer, and other animals. This connection enabled us to 'go forth and multiply'.

In North America, a natural short grass ecosystem exist that we call the Great Plains. The grasses that grow there are short because of the arid conditions that they must grow in. This is ranching country and the protein produced here is dependent upon grazing animals free ranging, and short grass that has a chance to grow seasonally when rain does occur. But those that live there do not always see the intimacy between competing exotic grasses, weather patterns, and the economics of grazing too many animals, let alone the ecology or history that seals their fate like Mesopotamia.

As we move eastward, we enter the mixed grass area where during wet years there are species of grass that grow taller. It is here we have chosen to make the grass shorter or concentrate on a single grass specie to feed the multitudes- wheat. How long can we produce this precious specie before the soil is changed forever? What is missing will probably be what is needed to produce those native grasses that originally created the soil.

As we move eastward further still, we enter an ecosystem and plant community what was once known as the Tall Grass Prairie. Here, the tall grass dominated the landscape and created and covered fertile soil up to thirty feet thick. Again, we have chosen to replace this prairie with many things. First and foremost, came the need to feed the world. The food we have chosen to grow is corn and we renamed the tall grass prairie the Corn Belt. This tall species is grown alone, evenly spaced, chemically protected, genetically altered, and cut at its base annually. We now have created the ultimate plant that can create generations of humans fed on corn - more than can be supported in a single valley in a lifestyle that was like the prosperity of the great valley of Mesopotamia at the beginning of civilization.

Little do we care that only patches of long grass prairie remain. It is ironic that the remains of prairies can often be found next to the well-kept short grass cemeteries. As eastern cities grew, landscape architectures looked to the cemeteries as models for creating parks. Landscapes of short grass and trees have now become a refuge to serve the living and the dead.

We have become a culture that seeks refuge in our own homes and yards. We rush from the city to our suburban home as fast as we can. We support massive road building projects to get there, whose right-a-way must be kept free of obstructions, so we plant and maintain more short grass areas. When we do get home, we spend most of our time maintaining our small patches of short grass with polluting gas driven vehicles and chemicals. Can you see the similarities of your single species of grass management in your yard and those in the corn field of your midwestern farmer?

In our zeal to make our homes and parks more natural we have created environments that are continuing to destroy nature and wildlife. Elm trees abounded in the eastern United States until decades ago, when we planted them side-by-side on every street boulevard. With this practice we created a Dutch Elm disease epidemic that has nearly eliminated the species in much of its range. Today we have created a new threat that accompanies our short grass mentality.

Gypsy moths are now destroying our eastern forest. Through research we have discovered the main predator of the moth's larval caterpillar is the white-footed mouse that inhabits our native grasslands. In replacing our grasslands and prairies with short grass and roadways devoid of this ferocious little predator we have literally created nurseries for the Gypsy moth. The urban environment we have created in our parks, playgrounds, and streets and suburbs of America now can affect eastern forest communities.

At what time will we realize in our efforts to maintain a single species – whether the human one or the short grass one - we are eventually destroying all others. Little do we realize that this lack of success in understanding what is happening will be the end of the assuming "thinking being" that separates him from the rest of the animal kingdom.

Wilderness and the Mind

True wild is wilderness. That is a fact. But the more man influences what was once wilderness the less he understands what it is; then the definition of wild takes on a warped meaning and man falls deeper into crags of his own demise- civilization.

Those geniuses that had the forethought, when man began to reduce the wilderness , to insist that there be places where man could only enter as a fellow animal, without the gadgets that became machines, and only for a short time so even the thoughts of changing it did not set root. They did a monumental task that today needs to be praised and brought to the forefront of the human mind and not forgotten. I do not hear much from the *Wilderness Society* anymore but know it is me who is out of tune.

Wilderness is in part of the mind fewer and fewer people perceive let alone visit. Even in my youth when I first experienced it, it was only a getaway, from the pressures of a youth becoming a man. After a visit to the wilderness and returning to civilization, only then I dimly aware of a peace that had settled upon the mind and body. Civilization was calling louder and there was to be no peace. Today, the tranquility of wilderness is so fleeting to most but those fortunate to have glimpses in their hearts can see their primitive self. Today, often the visit to the wilderness involves bringing all the implements and equipment to make the journey easier; the weight of the pack and its contents reduced for portages, or the weight of the vessel on the water, has been scrutinized to eliminate the effort of physical endurance during the visit. I can only hope these modern techno gadgets allow the visitor more time to sit in the wilderness to ponder life, its value, and find peace. The tan-colored or birch bark canoe has been replaced by the bright-colored kayak; I am not sure the human eye can filter out these aesthetic disturbances a water horizon of solitude.

I was fortunate to give the experience of wilderness my daughters with their first visit to a wilderness when they were 4 and 6 years of age. We visited the Sylvania Tract Wilderness on the UP Michigan/Wisconsin border for three days. The lake water was clear, and it was their first-time canoeing and fishing where they could see all what was happening to the very bottom. I could see wonder in their thoughts turning and expressions of wonder at this new experience ... what was dad getting us into now.

There were two aspects typical of a wilderness experience that occurred. These experiences I believe imprint on the human subconscious just as tragic events do, but with better direction for the future.

The first, was eyeing their first loon. Wilderness animals are rarely afraid and approach humans with curiosity and no fear as they do not know what they are. The loon dove and surfaced right at the bow of the canoe where they were sitting and the joy and wonder on their faces I will never forget.

The second, was a violent thunderstorm in the night with lightening striking all around us and echoing across the water for what seemed like forever. We huddled tightly in the tent. The next morning the sun shined brightly and all glistened with the wetness. After breakfast we headed home where we had to paddle to and then transverse a single short portage. The portage was lined with the tall majestic white pines, the symbol of Northwoods wilderness. At the beginning of the portage on the edge of the sandy lake we were leaving was a twelve-inch poplar tree that had been recently severed into two pieces at an angle by a huge sliver of wood that was now sticking in the ground at our feet. Looking up we found the sliver had been cut from a tall white pine above by a lightning bolt and propelled through the poplar below. It had happened in the night during the violent storm.

This is what wilderness does ... it humbles you to insignificance. The majesty of nature is at its peak ... undisturbed and calling to the primitive subconscious that this is the way the world was created and should remain. For the short time you are there, you experience the call of the wild where life   and death are hidden natural occurrences far from civilization where it is abhorred.   It needs to be preserved so we have places to use as living models as to what an ecologically proper world is.

Green and Silent Spring

When spring turns the landscape from the blindness of winter white to the dull brown of spring it is quickly spot-brushed green in the warm sun. The succession of green flows from the grasses to the shrubs to the trees with such a rush that this short season always appears to be jumping to summer. But those closest to the land know that this is the way of nature.

Those closer yet to the land see that there is a timing to this not based on air and soil temperature, or genetic codes hidden deep in root, seed, or embryo. It cannot be easily recorded or studied unless they can use the terms "lushness" or "harmony" in their scientific descriptions. The shades of the greens of spring could fill their own Crayola box and the descriptions of the complexity of interactions in nature in a small area could fill the memory of the largest computer. The cover supplied or not supplied by this early growth of vegetation must affect the brandishing of bird mating in spring. An attempt for every bird to display their territories and prowess, the bright color of the male and dull color of the female plumage. can be hidden by lush green foliage, or the sound of a bird song's harmony muffled by the same. Yet, the open silhouette of treetops and shrubs allow the clear melodies emitting from the highest perches give the early territories of the bluebird, cardinal, blackbird and meadowlark credence. The highest tree or shrub limbs, last to get foliage, now becomes important on whose territory this is and who is to mate with who.

Are many avian courtships stymied by the insect prey that have not joined this early spring scenario? Will this early rush to spring leave food lacking for their young in June? Or must the competition that once barely existed between species now come into play? On a walk the other day I saw a blackbird, meadowlark, and red-bellied woodpecker all feeding within a few yards of each other in a grass swale adjacent to a recently sprayed, fallow, no-till cornfield. This observation only creates more questions on the effects of loss of diversity; Were they feeding on organisms reacting to and fleeing the pesticide cocktail just applied to the adjacent field? Did they have a choice of their food source on this early spring morning.

Our perspectives on the natural world are changing as the scientist narrows in his specialties and the common man is more removed from the land by technologies and modernization. With increased pressures for economic development in agriculture and industry comes strident increases in destruction of the earth. One feels a hopelessness and solemn silence unless all are awakened to our plight. Climate change, global warming, and an early spring all have things in common – things are happening fast. We are not reacting to it because we are too busy to listen to the birds of spring.

The complexity of ecological interactions added to variations in season temperatures and moisture only confound finding the answers to these questions and a plethora of others. The most disheartening question to be answered is " will there be any one about on the landscape in the green springs of our future to ask – let alone – answer these complex questions. We all need to take a walk into nature and think about what is right.

The Nutrient Game

Whether we speak of food chains or food webs there is a channeling of nutrients from one organism to another. Which path it chooses is so little understood, but the paths are certainly affected by man. We have no sense of time and reason when viewing the path of nutrients, but we can stand mystified when we see people starving and droughts occurring. We are unable to recognize changes in the land until these negative changes are on the level we associate with an "Act of God".

The nutrient game begins with chemical elements becoming molecules as they are transformed by single-celled organisms on the way to higher life forms. Life has taken a giant leap from the heat of the sun to a plant produced by photosynthesis. The nutrient game should never end with a top predator as wolf, lion, leopard, killer whale, shark, muskellunge, or man ... all need to return to the soil or bottom ooze and begin the nutrient game at the start of the circular monopoly game again. What happens to the nutrients between these events needs to be understood by thinking man because it is his decisions in the future that will determine what will live, what will die, and which path of nutrients will be left. It is man's understanding of the interlocking sets of feedback loops of nutrients, in absence of greed, that will maintain the integrity of the natural world that supports all life.

We view this nutrient flow as an upward process with elements lodging in plants and animals were predation, consumption, or the end of the growing season marks death of the individual organism. Yet on the larger more complex scale of the community, several nutrient shifts can occur more slowly. But they do occur with changes in plant and animal species, water quality, and aesthetics. Most of these nutrient shifts in the past were unrecognizable because it took a single lifetime of an individual to view. An individual's comments on these changes in a natural community are viewed by our modern society as the ramblings of an old man on what the good old days were like.

For example, environmentalists and conservationists are quick to look at present land use practices in our watersheds to answer the water quality problems of today. Eroded and plowed land, poor land-spread waste handling practices, runoff from urban sprawl, and failing septic systems are the culprits of our water quality problems today, not a progression of changes in the nutrient flow through the webs and chains from land to water that have occurred just one hundred years into ancient times.

During pioneer days we built dams to provide power to process grain and timber into food and buildings. The removal of native vegetation and a canopy cover on the land, not only quickly brought water to the streams and lakes; but created a bare soil environment for non-native plants to establish themselves. As time progressed, we built more dams to regulate the flow of water that was coming too quickly off the land surface. In even later years we constructed smaller low head dams to stabilize water levels in the lake and prevent fish from leaving the lake during high water periods.

What happened during this process is the interlocking sets of nutrient feedback loops were lost. The canopy that protected the steep slopes and highly erodible soils of the glaciated Northland from spring rains and summer heat was lost. The plow and drain tile now feed the world but the understanding of the native plant nutrient feedback loop that created this soil is not understood- let alone considered for the future integrity of food production.

Do you believe that dams put in place to stop flooding until the canopy of trees grew back will ever be removed? At present the value of lake front property created by the dam or the power that it produces outweighs any ecological understanding of the destruction that it causes. Besides the power is needed to run the paper mills who do not want a restored forest canopy because young clear-cut aspen makes better paper.

The dams have prevented the movement of fish and other aquatic organisms that maintained the water quality as nutrient transporters. Bottom feeding fish, minnows, snails, and clams are all organisms that maintain our water quality through their feeding and filtering practices; yet their repopulation after gross pollution of the industrial revolution has been hampered by dams and other obstructions in our waterways. Is it a wonder that the aquatic plants that now dominate our waterways are those that can take nutrients from silt laden water and survive in water of low transparency? Further, we can complain about the "weeds" yet cannot attend a public hearing on dam relicensing.

At what point will our conscious minds recognize that progress without understanding the consequences on the natural world is but an undertaking of regression of the quality of life developed through natural history? As Leopold said biotic communities are too large, too complex, or too widely dispersed to be addressed by government conservation. It must be addressed by the private landowner. They must be able to discern that their small part of the land has the same big picture as the large biotic community that we must be part of.

The Power of Light

There is a shadow cast over mankind that the angle of the light is not the cause of. We do not walk straight and tall at high noon where the only shadow falls upon one's inner self. We cannot see a world when we worry only about our self, our family, and our country.

A competitiveness of man against man; one household having more than the next; and one nation stronger and more powerful than the next; is the mode of modern society. We have time and time again used the resources of this earth for the materialism, without considering what we are taking from the whole of this Planet Earth. We feel this planet's resources are inexhaustible and the rights of man includes manipulating them for his own benefit. The long shadow left is not the world as it was meant to be.

There is an energy that flows through all things on this earth. We categorize it in a formula 'as nothing can be created without something being destroyed". We transform elements from the resources of the earth into possessions that give use and power for a short time; then they become artifacts of this earth that archeologic history later reveals and human's wonder what happened. But during this short time on earth each society continues to make the same mistakes that eventually leads to its cultural downfall. When will the progress of man stand tall enough to lead the energy of light without casting a shadow?

The ills of man seem to be always linked to the extractions of resources beneath the surface of the earth: the greed of gold, the air pollution of oil, the radiation poisoning of uranium, the groundwater pollution of natural gas extraction. We only see the benefits that these earthly resources have brought to progress and wealth. We are now at a point where the resources above the surface of the earth; the powers of the sun, wind, and water can replace the problems of these power resources, so far, we hesitate and only come up with excuses as to why not.

The State of Our Resources

The year 2000 created two environmental reports on the state of Planet Earth and the state of the state we call home- Wisconsin. Our poor township has no such report - nor did we expect to produce one; in addition , if a report were to be written it would go unread, unnoticed, and unheeded by the majority in the township -as does the reports of the state and the world!

In October of the new millennium the first report of a four-million-dollar project known as the Pilot Analysis of Global Ecosystems (PAGE for short) was to be presented at a special session of the United Nations. This assessment gives the first comprehensive look at the five major types of ecosystems- forest, freshwater systems, coastal- marine habitats, grasslands, and agricultural lands. It is ironic that agriculture is considered a major ecosystem- as it is practiced: it is a major worldwide disruption of the land and not any type of sustainable environment of diversity. What

New York writer or world organization could make such a blatant error without interior motives or did they just get lost in anthropomorphic self-indulgence that man can create an ecosystem? Yet the preview of the report is correct enough to title its introductory article in large bold letters - CONDITION CRITICAL.

The state of Wisconsin's glossy publication *The State of our Natural Resources* steps up to the environmental plate with the opening quote in the sustaining ecosystem section saying "the states ecosystems are balanced and diverse. They are protected, managed and used through sound decisions that reflect long-term considerations for a healthy environment and a sustainable economy". This pep rally cheer is far from true - it is only an indication that we do not see the subtle loss of the intricacies that hold the land together, the fragmentation of it due to our needs, the disruptions because of lack of true understanding of interconnections.

Without any type of written explanation of the condition of the township we live in we were told, in a new state law, that by the year

2010 we were to come up with a land use plan that will protect the land. This law had been titled "Smart Growth" in a name that suggests perceptive economic progress that considers the effects on the land. What we probably were to come up with were toothless regulations that are meant to protect human rights to the land. In the end these laws would have divided what remains of the human community that once depended on the land for its sustenance. A few years later this law was repealed.

Why do people in the name of progress and prosperity changed the landscape without consideration for that what is natural. The edges between habitats of forests, wetlands, and grasslands have been modified and forgotten just as the animal species that viewed and traveled through them. Someday, we will be the forgotten specie of time, same as those records of land use management that were no longer heeded and stored in some forgotten file.

Yet, there is hope if an education is created that leads with this question "How will what I am about to do affect the land and if it does is there another way to do it that does not"? This basic principle can be expanded to every action if one understands that land encompasses all that is around us. Whether it is a product we receive from around the world or a product in our backyard - it is still from the land. There is a movement now along shorelines that any further development along its border must be accompanied by some sort of restoration of native vegetation. The combination of innovative conservation decisions and restoration will be fruitful to the land, but the educational system must be quickly modified to reflect these critical intentions.

The question is "How long will it take for this ecological education to develop a society of individuals that would humble themselves to be a member of the land community, and will we do it in time?

Time Scales

Time to each of us is different- but in most people's understanding it only spans our own life of seventy to eighty years. Our view of scale is often the progression of an increase in knowledge about the world around us and the drastic changes in our lives due to technology during that time. Most of us at best can also see into the lives of our parents and children another 40 years in either direction by just knowing their personalities and histories. But what ability are we creating with our knowledge over time to adjust to our place on earth?

We hear our grandparents or older generations describe what the land was like when they were young. The land is not like that today, so we often reflect that their memories of yesterday are not that clear and let it go at that. But the subtle changes of land in a single lifetime are important to understand; For these changes are secrets to the hidden changes of the past that need to be applied to the future of land management.

It is a coincidence that a forest typically has a similar time scale as humans. It takes from eighty to one hundred and sixty years-depending on where it is- to regenerate to a mature forest after clear-cut harvest. But recently researchers in the fast-growing southern hardwoods have found that there is a problem. When comparing old growth forest with little disturbance to clear cut areas adjacent, the species richness and total plant cover only came back at half and a third, respectively; even when the oldest recovery period of eighty-seven years was considered. The question in time scale is how many logging cycles will occur before there is no diversity or ground cover? What is the consequence to animals and weather? How long, if ever, will there be a recovery?

On the contrary, look at a forest fire prevention. In a single lifetime Smokey, the Bear had been successful in nearly eliminating forest wildfires caused by man and the most extraordinarily successful marketing campaign ever. Do forest fires eliminate diversity and species richness? Do forest fires create diversity and total plant cover on the longer time scale?

Without forest fires, an abundance of herbaceous woody vegetation accumulates, that is extraordinarily successful in transpiring water from the ground to the air. Water tables during the lifetime of many of my old friends have dropped considerably. Open water and wetlands are not recovering during the wet periods of the wet/ dry cycle, protracted drought may now be the norm. Have we now realized that with fire control what we have done for the good of all in the short term of a lifetime is detrimental to the good of all in the long run?

What we often gain in our lifetime is knowledge not wisdom. Wisdom creates an understanding that causes positive changes. For these changes to take place there must be actions. Today wisdom development in conservation and environmental issues is stifled by knowledge that is spread through a vast network of experts unable to bridge the connections we call ecology. Those few who can make the connection fail to get results as we have a world that is not listening or is too busy living their lives ... not the lives of their generations to come.

The great irony ... the greatest natural resource campaign of all time, Smokey the Bear cause, is now just a microcosm of the propaganda and media spins about the pros and cons of climate change and global warming effects ... changes so large in our global ecosystem disruptions that we need a much bigger, greater, and convincing advertising campaign for all the world to accept.

To Feed the World

It appears that since the time that man founded cities that his greatest concern was to feed those who cannot feed themselves. The resources of the land are there to do this and all other uses are secondary. But what have we really done in this single- minded cause?

The early civilizations all had their signature crop that made their population grow and become the "seats of civilization". China had its rice ... Mesopotamia had its wheat ... and Central America nearly had its corn or maize. In the case of Central America, the original maize was a smaller grain and not enough to sustain cities and they failed. It took centuries of low-key hybridization to come up with maize that could sustain a larger population. Probably a good thing for the Americas as it held off the destruction of land for a few centuries.

Have you ever asked why Mesopotamia "the land of fruit and honey" is now desert? Or why China's rural landscape cannot produce more food for its people or why their meals have always included clear soup (non-drinkable water)? The answer is "It is in the soil stupid". You cannot continue to take from it without giving back and protecting it. Somehow, we are slow learners on this very concept.

Scientist have identified the nutrients necessary to grow most plants. They have also followed these basic nutrients through crop plants and into various domestic animals. Yet in their methodical single-minded obsessions to target the specifics, they have not quite figured out the secrets of sustainable soil … to give back to it what was taken away by misuse … if there is no economic reason to do so. Unadulterated animal waste as a nutrient for soil integrity is a solution lost in agribusiness today.

We only must visualize what nature has offered in wilderness and the areas least affected by man's hand. We must look at it carefully, without the thoughts of economic gain, or how to change it to meet our needs. We must understand what nutrients are present and how they move from one living organism to another and eventually back to feed the original plant or animal. Did you know it takes over fifteen years to make an area a wilderness in the United States? How long do you think it will take to understand what makes a wilderness sustain itself; therefore, giving us a clue on how we should approach sustainability and the ecological connections that make it work, then apply it our food production needs before it is too late.

Do we need to do this with every intact ecosystem? I suspect not, as I believe there are common threads in this sustainability thing. We just need to observe and learn. Once we see the threads, we can apply them. We need both plants and animals on the landscape that were meant for the soil and climate conditions. Ones that developed over time ... ones that evolved there. Look at the life histories and ecology of natives ... the plants, the insects, the animals. With these close observations understanding methods of protecting their interconnections will evolve.

Forget the genetic engineering, the industrialized farming, and synthesizing of the product produced. Look for the sustainability in the detail of what is natural. For instance, the recent panic over the recent decline in the monarch butterfly population was blamed on the agricultural pesticides by many conservation groups. Knowing the importance of milkweed species of plants as the needed host plants for reproduction of the monarch, why would one not look to its destruction and loss as an ecosystem failure as an obvious reason? Yes, these plants have been sprayed with chemicals and the prairie and wetland ecosystems that support them have been eliminated by industrial agriculture ... "get rid of the fence rows so I can farm more land as those box elders there just broke my mirror on my $300,000 combine". "I need new drain tile as my 4-wheel drive, eight-wheel tractor almost got stuck near the swamp hole."

Do not think about the farmland that was once wetland and prairie plants - that produced the soil- that you are dependent upon to produce the monoculture crop ... and pay for the combine and the tractor! Do not think about sustainable ways to feed the world and let us continue to remove and disturb sustainable nature that we owe life to!

Consider the need for native pollinators. The recent honeybee pollination crisis has experts scrambling for reasons and justifying causes. Yet the solution, just as with the monarch butterfly and other insects is obvious. But what can we do about the giant industrial machines we have created to feed the world? Things will be OK as the honeybee was not part of the original pollination equation in our Americas and the pest problem is being solved by GMO crops. Right consumers! Cancer is our right and a few less people is not the solution! Right!

Too Many is Not Enough

There is one irony in this world that cannot be ignored. Wilderness and civilization. There never will be again a more perverse and reverse situation than what man is doing to this place that supports him. Wilderness has always given way to a wrongheaded man that has never learned through the eons of time ... wealth in wilderness terms is contrary to poor in humanity terms. Wilderness has always been a place of plenty and in our warped senses of what is important in life in time we continue to destroy it.

From the two cradles of civilization in Mesopotamia and Eastern China that were once wilderness we have created a desert of the former and traffic jams that last weeks of the later. Another cradle of civilization that failed, Central America, mocking the others has reverted to jungle. Could it be that the fate of mankind lies in understanding that?

wilderness is important? Wheat and rice came from the wilderness as a staple that created civilization. Central American corn needed time and genetic manipulation to catch on before supporting our world of too many. This pandemic of people and their technologies now have not only spread over much of the supporting land surface but now affect the places where we only once passed through ...... the water and the air. Still in our hardheaded absurdity to survive and compete we have not learned enough is enough. Wilderness is our salvation.

Why is it that when we observe plenty, we must have it until it is gone? Being an American our values that created an independent democracy came from depending on this land that was once a wilderness. The ironies since our beginning is overwhelming. First, the keystone species of the vast wilderness land of the west, the buffalo, was destroyed in a blink of a civilized hunger for meat and robes to survive the cold, shortly followed by the devastation of the prairie to feed our greed for more meat and corn syrup. Second, the keystone specie of the sky, the passenger pigeon, was shot in a cause of bringing a delicacy to our hungry needs and maybe ironically there was not room for them in the skies...... and airplanes. Now we venture to the last wilderness in North America, the Arctic tundra where we are willing to sacrifice the last herds of plenty, the caribou, for a need of an industrialized world civilization for coal, oil, and natural gas. Will greed always create insurmountable odds that a land ethic cannot overcome? A democracy must have open space and wilderness to survive from being poor morally and ethically.

Understanding and Survival

Survival of man in the past was dependent on many things. Today, that survival of man now depends even more on the same things, but the list has been expanded because we have gained knowledge with time. Tomorrow, man's survival will depend on the survival of understanding of the knowledge he has gained through history, and a universal ethic that comes with this understanding that the survival of all things is essential.

Air, Water, Food .... These are the basics of survival that we have now codified in survival training for humans. If we look closely beyond human needs these basics generally extend to all living things. Though we take these things for granted there is a dual timeline that we must connect. The survival code for these basics say we can only live three minutes without air, three days without water, and three weeks without food. These are painful facts that few humans in the civilized world ever experience until our bodies give up at death unless a tragic mishap of violence, poor planning, or sheer stupidity has created these timeline situations.

It is essential to understand that time repeats itself in both scale and universal context. This is what all organisms on this planet will face, and it will be tragic and painful, if we do not use our knowledge of life to act with wisdom to save all.

Too Much of a Good Thing

Let us address the benefits and problems that are created by excess. The list of benefits and problems is long. But the excuses for not addressing these benefits and problems is short. Satire may show justification for the solutions.

Take obesity. It is good for the economy. It is led by shopping for and eating poor food choices, while we are in the store, we buy more things than we need ... just to feel better about our woes. Because of this human malady we will suffer throughout our lifetime ... the medical and insurance companies will flourish trying to make us feel better. We probably will die younger stemming the tide of over population and take the pressure off our Planet Earth that provided the resources for our earlier shopping and eating excesses. Is it the destruction of the self or the planet that has got you down? I am sure you are more aware of self.

Take technology. Again, it is good for the economy. That phone that once sat in your living room for a lifetime now gets to ride along with you and is replaced every year or two. The copper wire infrastructure of yesterday's telephone has been replaced by cell towers and satellites. What a boom for construction companies and high-tech industries to fill the skies and horizons with more wires and flashing things in the night skies. This is great for birds and bats during migration. They can be killed by running into the communication towers and do not have to make the long flights anymore. Their food of biting insects can flourish and can spread disease to all. Star gazing astronomer and other viewer now have additional wonders to keep them alert at night with satellites they no longer will have to ponder the origin of the universe but wonder who put those objects in the night sky.

Take plastic. It has made our life so convenient. Plastic food and drink containers can battle for space on the store shelf, in the cupboard, and the landfill. Plastic floats. Plastic shopping bags of our global economy have created a new island, soon to become a continent, in the middle of the Pacific. Plastic can replace anything. A three-dimensional printer is ready to duplicate into my new my hip bone ... I always wanted to be a superhero bionic man ... it is a good start. Plastic lasts forever, we need to plan for this by creating a new recycling jingle, "do not compost when you can get the most out of plastic forever".

Obesity and buying things we do not need are problems of excess in the affluent societies we live in. These two problems seem to come from the same unconscious source. Do we shop, eat, and consume in excess to replace the happiness that is missing from our lives and homes? Do we eat convenience foods or make purchases because we have the money or lack the energy or motivation to cook or create things that we really need to have a healthy and happy life? A humanity of privilege can create vanity, greed, and create laziness!

What Will Save Us?

There seems some urgency to solve the problem of what man has done to the Planet Earth that now threatens all life. In our rush to solve our energy and environmental crisis, we are shifting technologies into high gear that will give us energy for the short run but causes long run destruction of our planet. Natural gas extraction by "fracking" in the open plains of Wyoming was one thing, now doing the same in the forested lands of the East coast or Canada is another. The usurping of environmental laws for quick profit and lobbying for government regulation shortfalls in these times seems to be the norm – quick fixes at the cost of the environment.

Has it always been this way; the monetary system and economy run by the politics of NOW? Will we learn in time that the earth's ecosystems can only handle so many disruptions before life as we know it ceases? To understand something this important must infiltrate all of societies and nations. The question must be asked, "Can this be done in time?"

I remember discussions regarding land ethics over 30 years ago on how to save this world from man's greed of material and economic gain. These discussions were a result of the pondering of Aldo Leopold's writings regarding a need for a 'land ethic'. The discussion always fell to whether laws or a deep ethic of caring for the land and not wanting to destroy it was the way to go. As naive as we were, we could see that laws could be changed or ignored or that human greed would find a way to usurp any law.

Therefore, a silent race began to create a land ethic in our youth that could be carried into the future. The field of environmental education was born to instill these necessary values into our society. At the same time technology, consumerism and "need for a bigger and better life" infiltrated our culture completely. This silent race is being won by the latter, as it has pulled man so far from the land and out of the perspective of how important our natural world is to survival.

We have created a society of immediate wants and a short attention span. Environmental education still tries to play on our innate instincts to be drawn to the outdoors and nature while joining the technology of this society where videos and media are needed to get any message to our youth. At the same time the direction of education focuses on meeting the demands of the technical and digital aspects of our modern society. Popular cuts in school budgets seem to stop or reverse any gains in the environmental education... a land ethic can be lost before it has a chance to be developed in our youth.

Conservation Futures

What is conservation today? Is it fund raisers to operate conservation organizations aimed at maintaining certain species? Is it the environmentalists constantly screaming "Save the Earth"? Is it government programs that protect the resources? Or is it landowners trying to preserve what is dear to them? It appears to be a blend of all - each facet of conservation trying to influence others for their cause. We often go about each of these conservation activities uninformed of what we are putting our efforts towards or the true consequences of our actions. Just as time is relative to perspective, time will be the judge of our efforts. We are slowly advancing in all these conservation enterprises to the habitat level that is basic to general preservation.

The duck, pheasant, grouse, trout, bass, muskie, deer, and elk hunting fraternities and the whale, mountain lion, bird, wolf, manatee, and snow leopard sororities are now realizing that their efforts in conservation and preserving what they want is tied to the habitat of hundreds of other organisms.

New organizations are forming that now specializing in saving and restoring a specific disappearing habitat such as prairie or river. And even newer are organizations moving towards the management of exotics. Is this a progression of man's ability to understand the land?

Those environmentalists, whose penchant for stopping resource use, need to take a step into the opening of man's influence that has existed for tens of thousands of years. It is only after living on our own, too removed from the edge of the wild, do we charge back to it demanding that we should leave it alone. Little do they realize, if their partiality for wilderness was instead set for restoration in their own back yard, that their seventh generation would view it as such.

Government conservation has moved out of the arena of what we can see. The main efforts seem to focus on contaminants in our air, earth, and water in a world of parts per billion whose chase to protect the resources is so high tech and expensive only politicians who are used to spending money without true long-term insight can support. The real solution is in the return to understanding microbiology of the natural world that will eventually lead the way to solving these unseen disturbances. This micro revolution is paralleled in the seeing world of fish, forest, wildlife ecology, by understanding the need for innovative restoration techniques that let us grow in the knowledge of what once was in the wild and abandoning much of our traditional management techniques.

Private lands have the best chance of long-term preservation, but are overrun by government officials, environmentalists, and single-species conservation groups looking for restrictions or access. Yet, chances for private land natural resource protection and restoration dwindle each year that taxes increase, and the pace of our modern society keeping owners from finding a peace in their own back yard.

We have left nature management mostly to the politicians. It is they who make the laws and appropriate the money for the conservation in America today. It is they who react quickly to the short-sighted views of land conservation as they may not be around for the next election. It is the politician that hear the proposed solutions of conservation by government conservation organizations, the environmental lobbyist, and the outdoor recreationist in the halls of congress and cocktail parties. But when will the Savanna Congress be held in the openings created by fire between the forests and restored prairie where they can take the time to evolve the true spirit and solutions of what conservation needs to be?

Do Not Forget to Apply the Sunscreen

The vivid scientific discovery that sunscreen washed off our silky skin into our oceans has decimated our ocean coral reefs is a welcome relief. It is relief to know it is not the depletion of the ozone layer due to carbon emissions and climate change that is going to cause starvation and water wars that will be our demise. Now we can stop using sunscreen, stay out of the sun, and help China's mass industrialization produce a zillion more plastic beach umbrellas to be shipped around the world on those diesel fuel sucking cargo ships. Besides, that is why we put the sunscreen on ... to avoid skin cancer ... so we do not perish a slow death as an individual. We might just as well be selfish and mess up this Planet Earth and have all species suffer too and ... of course, share in a slow painful death.

The ocean is so large that destroying these coral reefs is no big deal. The massive floating islands of plastics in the middle of the Pacific that are twice the size of Texas is no big deal either. What would we do with all that plastic anyway? Maybe these plastic islands are replacing ocean life habitat lost from our loss of the reefs due to a chemical in sunscreen? Plastic and 3D printing can reproduce anything, can't it? How about plastic replacing calcium carbonate that is found in our own bones, the bones of fish that feed us, or even duplicate the coral reefs, since the plastic islands and in the Pacific Ocean already?

The depletion of our ocean fisheries by overfishing is no big deal. The largest population in the world, China, whose cultural cuisine for thousands of years has been fresh fish reared with rice on the rural landscape has moved the populations to cities. In these cities near coastal waters, China is replacing traditional fish diets with bushel baskets of corn dried in the upper Midwest of the United States and hauled in shipping containers using diesel-belching cargo ships. With a higher standard living urban Chinese can now buy fish from the depleting ocean fishery, depleted by habitat loss that of course includes coral reef. Now, we can replace the ocean fishery losses with aquaculture that uses fish meal from the fish forage base of the ocean, or the corn shipped from America. No problem! Right!

Maybe one should not pick on China or India for their population-related problems and for loss of coral reefs and ocean habitat. We are bent as a species to increase our standard of living which is tied to moving to the city. A concentration of people must discharge their treated waste someplace. Whether it is the Mississippi, the Ganges, or rivers that flow to the South China Sea these discharges and their micro contaminants end up in the island vacation spots we find peaceful and pristine. Then these new wealthy city dwellers will be able to afford a vacation to the Indo-Pacific rim or the Caribbean where blue water hides dead coral reefs, and it is no longer safe to swim or sunbathe on the beach. Instead, maybe, we could promote vacations to the quaint old bed and breakfast farmsteads of the U.S. Midwest corn belt, but it is no longer there as it has been bulldozed to plant a few more rows of corn.

I Love My Car

We Americans are trained young to love our automobiles. In the beginning if you did not have wheels you were not cool ... and "cool" is one of those most used words in the English language ... of course next to the word "car".

Just less than a century ago walking was the greatest means of getting around. You walked to school to work to play. You walked with your friends, your colleagues, and family. There were more paths through the woods, dirt roads, and even a few sidewalks in the city. People got sidetracked, lost, and found by new friends, and even met people by saying "hello" on this journey. We appreciated the simple things of quietness and aesthetics of nature along the way. Our need for speed was fulfilled by the bicycle that did not go so fast that one still could say "hello" and view the scenery.

But again, eventually, we had to get that license and drive to school. The "cool" then created a penchant to work the rest of our lives to buy a "cooler" and "faster" car. But then, our fathers made us aware of the responsibilities of maintenance, insurance, and providing gas for it ... we became a part of the American Dream. Wallah! The auto, oil, and insurance industries thrived to meet our lifetime needs. Thank you, baby boomers you created the keepers of the Fortune 500 stock corporations and did not even know it.

So, what kind of monsters did we create with the advent of our car passion. A need for steel, oil, insurance, roads, wealth, luxury, and greed ... just to name a few. And yes, let us not forget the environmental consequences: pollution, habitat destruction, and their many forms from as many sources. Are they monsters of economic growth and stability or roads to our slow extinction?

The simple pleasures of walking, scenic beauty, quiet times, and the time to really have a conversation with a person passing by are now what we seek in our spare time which is limited by the amount of time we must spend earning enough for the monsters above. The price of that car has steadily increased to a point where decisions are made to have a house roof ... or a sunroof ... for you cannot have both ... but you must have a car. The industry says the price is the consumers fault as he is demanding the luxury, technology, and convenience items. The question is really "who is driving who"?

So, the economy takes a tank because we still want the luxury home and the car ... and the monsters still want to make us happy and their stockholders happy, so they make sure we have the opportunity. Then everyone is in financial trouble and that car must last a few more years and humble pie must be eaten someplace. "But who is to eat the pie" says the government? Is it the financial industry, the auto industry, or the taxpayer and citizen with the older car?

Forget the long-term savings and survival, we need new cars and homes and a means to finance them .... our recovery is based on the social need for more possessions so let us go for it. Forget the long-term health and environmental woes that accumulate along with our possessions. We will let our children ride in new Subaru, Toyotas, and Volkswagens and not worry about their future of just being happy and at peace.

Human Identity Qualms

Man seems to be having an identity crisis in this modern world of too many people and high-speed communications. Perhaps it is because an individual is lost in the hordes of humans who have lost direction as a civilization and are finding their identity by attaching their name to the most successful tribe ... and there are a lot of tribes to choose from.

Where at one time the visual stimulus for man was the beauty of nature and that of another human through direct viewing and eye-to-eye contact. Technology has changed the simple shuttered box camera to today's plethora of communication devices. These ever-changing electronic driven apparatuses have driven the individual perspective of life into high-speed shuttering of a hyper mind. These communication devices have become portals for commercialization of all living things.

A thinking man once received knowledge from time spent in a quiet library where his own thoughts could be heard as words were lifted from the page by his own interpretation. This man is now a relic and recluse as he shuns the technology and is declared senile in respect to his reading, analyzing, and referencing a book when he could much easily Google for the answer that has all the thought completed for him.

A modern human is no longer identified by simply being a species let alone representing a gender for the species and must be politically correct. A modern 'person' has no gender, personality, or character flaws in fear of being labeled; biased, sexist, or racist. Is this an attempt to correct the monsters we have created through the modern media promotion of beauty, wealth, and power?

The modern world of electronic technology and mass media corresponds to a massive disconnection to the natural world. Not only do the masses of humans, now mainly linked through cell phones, iPad, and other forms of computers, connect less face-to- face, also uses the same devices and other machines to separate themselves from experiencing nature directly. The pastime of communing with nature from hiking, hunting, fishing, wilderness exploring, and wildlife viewing is being replaced by a video world of documentaries, reality gaming, and video reality shows.

What is replacing our early primitive instincts and heritage of the comradery of hunting, fishing, and gathering of food as a tribe or the sacred possession and respect of the products and the spirits of nature? It has been replaced by allegiances to a sport, and a brand of commercial snack food or beer to carried and shared at a crowded event or television facsimile, and a penchant to purchase gadgets and paraphernalia with the logo of their favorite sports tribe.

Part 3: TO GET IN STEP FOR OUR CHILDREN

Archeology and Ecology in the Future

Does modern science and data collection have the answers to solve our dilemmas of human's self-destruction of the earth ecosystems? The answer to this question remains to be seen and if we are to explore solutions to this quagmire, we must explore the ancient past. It would be wrong to run in the wrong direction to solve a problem and stumble only to land on one's face at future time that is too late to save our planet from us.

Drill cores in our ice caps has yielded ancient climate data and modern proof to what humans have done to our atmosphere since the industrial revolution. This physical and chemical scientific study set off more questions and more modeling on the biological world of the past trying to gain knowledge of cause and effect. All is good.

Science is filled with life-long personal expeditions that gain knowledge of the fossil record of man, flora, and fauna that is present now or became extinct in the past. We are even now gaining evidence of mass extinctions as well as smaller extinctions that may be related to changes in climate. But have we considered all with an ecological bent? We need to create data base with a goal of connecting ecosystem patterns of the past. If we collectively connect the natural histories of extinct and prior living organisms to their physical, chemical, and biological presence the mysteries of life on this earth will be easier to see in the future. One great lesson of history is that it seems to repeat itself with a twist.

Is this archeological-ecological approach the answer to global acceptance of solutions to the harsh reality that life could be ending on this Planet Earth as we see it? Both man's origin and primate extinctions, even during unpopulated times may have anthropologic keys to cooperation or non-cooperation needed for us to succeed in these modern times of too many people.

Common Threads

If you pay attention as you age and do not get sidetracked by the complexity of today's life, many things can become clear. A professional career of thirty years seems like a long time to some, but it is only a short time that can give you the experience to move towards wisdom the rest of your life.

The study of nature is particularly bent on this pattern of human endurance. The expert that specializes in one aspect of nature or a single organism has spent their career trying to understand interrelationships so complex that after thirty years there are more questions than answers. This professional often ends up feeling as if he has spent time crawling in a long culvert and is now come to the end of it where the light and openness brings wisdom to his gained knowledge and one wants to share it - but often one is tired and yearns the simple pleasures of retirement.

The study of an ecosystems is a study in time and change. For an example, the lakes on the granite bedrock of the Canadian Shield in the Northern Hemisphere have common geological history and similar human history; but slight geological variations and small human effects since the last ice age has created distinct characteristics. Fifteen thousand years ago in Wisconsin, after the glaciers receded, lakes were similar as a cold climate and raw earth limited diversity and production, but the geographic location on the local geographic and micro-climates sent them on different biological paths. As the climate warmed - and species recolonized from river waterways and uplands from the south - production and diversity of plant and areas developed differently and both productivity and diversity were limited. Some became shallow lakes and wetlands. The entrance of man upon the landscape brought changes to each lake just as wilderness gave way to the pioneer.

Overharvest of fish was probably one of the first manmade disturbances of these balanced but dynamic ecosystems. Fish in shallow water were easily captured at the time of spawning and was one of the earliest human practices of sustenance. Continual seasonal reduction of the top predator species set off ecological chain of events in lakes and rivers. In less than 150 years of too much civilization reversed the twelve to fifteen thousand years of developing diversity. Limited nutrient cycled through plants and animals of the lake community because of its great diversity adjusted this fish removal. Wild rice would be plant that traveled through the same scenario. This was a minimally disturbed natural community. Many nutrients accumulated in shallow lake and river systems and became open wetlands and closed forest. Overtime to many lakes and their watersheds have been negatively impacted by humans effecting the lake's ability to ecologically function and cycle nutrients.

A true understanding of an ecosystem where we can make decisions that will restore the diversity is yet to come. We have created specific sciences to understand many components of ecosystems, yet we have not created a system to bring the information together and use it. Using logic and our empirical knowledge to understand an ecosystem we will find that biological time repeats itself on different time scales. Whether it be: growth patterns based on predator- prey relationships; wet-dry cycles in weather; or the succession of any biological communities, these spatial sequences once collected as connect functions of an ecosystem will give us answers to the preservation and maintenance of our ecosystems to preserve all life on this Planet Earth.

Community Tinkering

When we think of community, we perceive a place where people live, communicate, and function. It is a society or civilization of man's fellowship with place. As humans we belong to many communities at the same time; a church, a club, a village, a city, a nation, a place called Planet Earth. Little do we understand the true community that allows all these communities to exist - the ecological community.

We are getting to know the parts of this large ecological community and how various parts function, but we continue to severely disrupt its function. Our tinkering with the ecological populations is likened to a predator that plays with it prey before it kills it. We will indeed kill it for our own greedy needs; but is it instinct or do we have a consciousness that can do without the killing? Is the survival of the humanity and all community dependent upon this consciousness?

We have passed laws to protect ourselves, other animals, and now we are passing laws to protect a few plant species. There has been a time scale for the acceptance of each protection, during which in the interlude life is still lost- but moralities have developed. Will these ethics develop further in man before he destroys all that supports him? Will he go beyond laws and understand that all life has worth as important as his own? Is this the same benefit that breaths life from one organism to the next?

The understanding of cause and effect in the ecological community cannot be entirely dependent upon a scientific approach in today's world. We do not have the time or luxury for scientific explanation and justifications to lead to actions for ecological corrections of our disturbances. Money, economic progress, and politicians have little desire or ethical motivation to face ecological collapses. We already have empirical evidence on living organisms and their ecological communities that can be used to create awareness for timely action now.

The answer is not in the complexity but in the simple and imaginative. If we can take a child's imagination and expose it to the natural community around him early enough in life- this imagination will mature into an understanding of a sustainable and healthy ecological community.

A sense of nature is still within us, yet our modern lifestyles and mechanics of living drives us farther from the ecological community that our ancient ancestors developed in. This is a consciousness of the whole planet's collection of individual communities- an unconscious realization that needs to be imprinted in all of mankind.

Diversity Restoration

There are two truths of biodiversity. The first, as you go from the equator to the poles the number and diversity of species decrease due to the cold and dryness. The second, on an island only so many species can survive, the smaller the island the smaller number of species. For every 10-fold increase in size of the island the species numbers double. We have applied these two principles to create models in understanding the biomass and number of species. The new question in biodiversity is, how do we apply these principles to gain back species we have lost?

First, we must understand the ecological matrix of an ecosystem that is undisturbed-true wilderness. It is framework we must understand for restoration to work. Are there examples of every type of wilderness communities from the equator to the poles? Do these wilderness examples represent all species or have some already been lost?

In the tropics we cannot agree on how many species are being lost daily, monthly, or yearly. In the temperate regions we have given up on biodiversity as the disturbance of man now reaches to the edges of the widespread wildernesses – ecological fragmentation is the norm. In the tundra and arctic there is wilderness because it is too harsh of climate for man and the resources extraction limited by diversity and weather. It is the temperate area that wilderness pattern will be hard pressed to surely understand.

An analysis in 1972 in the United States revealed that of the nation's 261 ecotypes, 157 are included in the National Wilderness Preservation System. Should we not be concerned in developing a plan to restore these other 104 ecotypes? In the temperate region of lost biodiversity, the restoration mode must be designed using our understanding of the small islands that still exist of native habitat. We have coined a term 'pre-settlement vegetation' ... relatively undisturbed plant community remnant components least effected by man as a starting point. If we take these islands and begin understanding the web of diversity remaining, we will soon learn how our disturbances have affected them. Through this process the edge around this island will be found to influence the island. As our understanding of the disturbances of the edge increases, restoration of the edge will follow increasing the size of the island. Our success of adding species that once were there, of course, will be dependent on size of the island. The goal in a time scale should be to connect several islands that have small differences in specie composition and diversity or represent an ecotype. Then the magic of the resiliency of nature and biodiversity restoration begins. It is then the pestilence of environmentalism finally has a base to grow on.

The role of studying the exotics of these remaining native plots is a key to the rehabilitation. How the exotic has become a part of the community and what it has replaced may be a key to the restoration. The understanding of the exotic on the edge of the disturbed native community may also be an important part of the true restoration. To eliminate or control the exotics on the edge will allow the observer to know the influences of community expansion or contraction. It allows those that see the opportunity to teach others the specific why of habitat loss not just the colloquialism of the word 'disturbance'. This a role for citizen scientists. Once these techniques are perfected the connecting islands and the growth of biodiversity can begin.

Be it 400 years or 15,000 years of disturbance, we only have a short period to utterly understand the causes or losses to biodiversity. Habitat destruction from population increases and natural resource consumption are accelerating, and we need to create an atmosphere in our collective consciousness that realizes the importance of the natural. The power to observe what is happening to nature and relate it to natural history is a key. As we grow older, and realize we will not live forever, it is natural to be inquisitive about our own human heritage. Is it not natural, as man ages on this earth, that he must concern himself with the natural history that supported him?

In this curiosity we must question what we have done to change natural history. For an example, we have found fire important in grassland and prairie restoration, but modern-day fire control policies are indeed a disturbance to natural communities- thanks to our successful conservation efforts of fire prevention developed the last 75 years. We have asked the question "Under what conditions did natural fire occur before the native cultures set fire to the prairie and what effect did, they have in changing or maintaining the community?" What role did fire have in the forest community or the wetland/lake community? Does the periodic presence of fire and its effect on the landscape effect hydrologic cycles to include ground water levels? What species thrive after a fire and what role do, they play in regenerating the community? What evasive exotics entered the picture after fire control entered the picture? But this is just one in the hundreds of practices and effects that humans have unwittingly wrought on the diversity of time.

If a species is removed or added what is the reaction of the ecosystem? Ultimately, we must ask what would happen to the ecosystem if man was removed from it. By asking this question and searching for the answer maybe then we may find a role on earth as advocators of biodiversity.

Eco-scaping

Our degree of recognition of the reasons for loss of species on this planet now is to be categorized into four main disturbance areas: habitat destruction, alien species, pollution, and overexploitation. The generalness of these categories is as non-descriptive as our solutions to stop these disturbances. We often know the individual specie is disappearing, as is the community, but our management to stop this act or define the exact cause of the act is not progressing to a point that we can save the community let alone the species.

If we continue to seek protection of biodiversity by protection of wildlands through purchasing and boundary designation will we fail in the end? If we continue to view disturbances in the natural landscape as fragmentation, will we also fail to protect the land in the end? We must view human disturbances as natural disturbances but channel the disturbance to restoration through human understanding and management. For an example, a plowed field, creates many characteristics of a hot fire. A drained or ditched wetland has many of the same effects as drought. These can be looked upon as short-termed disturbance that can be management.

At the same time, we have given the name "plant community" to situations we have created. For instance, the grassland community we call a sand barren. Most sand barrens are artifacts of the disturbance we caused by trying agriculture on a dry sand prairie. There is not one community today that has not been affected by a disturbance that can be directly or indirectly cause by man's presence on the landscape. Why do we spend time creating subcategories? Our energies spent on inventorying and categorizing could be spent on direct work on the disturbed lands. Our current approach is that of a politician - we will only be on the landscape for a short while, so our decisions must show results while we are here. Yet, restoration does not work that way. Those experts, who have no clue to the long-term results, seek security in short term results even if in the long term their accomplishments were not important.

Predators, parasites, and diseases can give clues that an ecosystem is out of sync. Competition from the same species, competing species, or exotics is also a complicated ecological mechanism that also effects a population. We spend so much time trying to define the parameters that effect a single organism in a population where we should be keying our management objectives on these indicators and how they interact with the community population.

We have a habit of defining communities as continuums in time that we must preserve. We call for their preservation knowing well that time will accommodate their successional trek and most of them will eventually turn themselves into some other community. We battle over the use of fire to stop the successional trek and look towards plant control grazing and manmade alternatives to preserve them. Yet, we could spend more time on man's compatibility with the land. We need to look at land management strategies that allow the land to contribute to the ecological integrity but also to the economic stability.

We try to manage the edge of these communities and expand the range of endangered species and habitats. At this edge we will manage to reduce competition from other communities, habitat destruction, and exotics that limit the expansion of the range. Yet we do not understand the continual flux and change in the present range. Long term weather changes affect the characteristics of this edge more than our attempted management. Our disturbances on a global scale are likely to affect the not only the small communities but large ecosystems by shifting the communities geographically. The threat to endangered habitats could be destroyed by global effects of man on climate.

Many plant species overlap communities or are always present in the transition of one community to the next. Their populations fluctuate with the climate effects of moisture, light, and temperature plus their ability to compete with other plant species - especially exotics. It is the disturbed areas created by man that provides the habitat that creates the advantage of exotics over native species at the edge of communities.

If we do not concentrate on restoring disturbed areas and planting edges of natural communities with native species, when greater climatic changes occur the loss of remaining native habitat could be a total loss. Therefore, former range boundaries of communities identified by pre-settlement habitat are not adequate in recognizing ecosystems that must be protected.

When the greater effects of global warming occur the integrity of our soil will be threatened the most, our ability to adjust to these climatic changes will be based on our ability to protect and restore these soil characteristics now.

Ecosystem Survival

All ecosystems are a collection of smaller parts that function individually and with increased complexity function cooperatively. These systems function and fluctuate with disturbances until these turbulences are so great that the system no longer functions. Now the smaller parts are again left to function individually at a reduced capacity for cooperation. Many of the ecosystems of the Planet Earth have been destroyed or have been so severely disrupted that the functioning of the entire biosphere is in jeopardy. What approaches can we take to restore the functioning of an ecosystem? Any approach must be integrated into the society as a long-term ethic for the development of sustained restoration and preservation of the plant communities that make up the ecosystems.

A local ecosystem needs to be redeveloped for the recognition and expansion of original vegetation that existed before the influence of man on a landscape. This system must be integrated into the local culture through environmental education in the school system. Identification and understanding of pre-settlement vegetation; plant successions, animal habitat, and the species that it supported would be the goals of this education beginning at the elementary level. Inventorying and restoration techniques as a part of secondary education curriculum.

These educational techniques would then be applied to the land at the township level. Assessments of the land would be made on the square mile basis and a current inventory of changes and improvements would be maintained in the town hall. Residents and landowners would have access to this information and the town hall would be the center for education, cooperative meetings, and planning the expansion of areas containing native vegetation.

Cooperation between landowners would be essential in the expansion of isolated patches of native plants through corridors and connection to other isolated plant patches until local plant communities once again become established. Techniques such as exotic and evasive species control, forest management, prairie burns, or others based on the individual plant community needs could be practiced in a more economic and effective manner through local resident and landowner cooperation.

Gathering and banking of native plant species seeds would be integrated into the school curriculum and township restoration. Annual harvest, sharing, and planting would be coordinated through an annual fall township gathering where expanded plant community boundaries would be recorded at the town hall. Fall harvest festivals with a new twist!

New residents and landowners in the township could visit the town hall that would become an interpretive center for the township's natural resources. Topography, soil, land use, and water resource information would be accessible to all. Protection and restoration strategies to resource problems can be addressed through an educational awareness created through the town center cooperation.

The functioning of an ecosystem must be addressed at this grass roots level in a community to show residents the results of a local effort that will eventually be felt globally. This will create an environmental ethic that will increase the understanding of sustainable land that will support us if we give nature a chance through restoration.

Ego Ecology

Aldo Leopold stated, "The problem of having an ecological conscious is that we live in a world of wounds". To make a living or have a "good life" we inadvertently create vast wounds on the land. Whether you are a farmer, miner, or a consumer progressing towards an improved standard of living you have raised havoc with our natural world. All products come from the land and the more people on earth the more we despoil our own nest.

We have come to a point where any self-healing mechanism of the biotic world, a balance that is normally self-correcting, will no longer sustain the pressures of man. We must change our ways.

The ego of man is tied to self: A self that must reproduce, flourish and bear children and increase their welfare beyond your generation's standard seems to be the theme of our modern culture today. Happiness is tied to having possessions for you and your family. For thousands of years philosophers have expounded that this is not true, that peace, tranquility, and "sense of place" is what brings happiness beyond the necessities of food, clothing, and shelter.

It is ironic that in the developed world our striving for these simple necessities we have reached way beyond the basics. Food is no longer meat, grain, fruit, and vegetables gathered from the orchard, garden, field, and forest. It is over processed, over packaged, and shipped great distances to meet our wealth of excess self-ego. Shelter has met the same level of indulgence. Instead of sharing living space we have created spaces for "self" and specialization. Private bedrooms, bathrooms, offices, theaters, and large spaces that provide shelter but may have a view of the natural through large windows that protect us from it is perceived uncontrolled seasonal malice. Clothing has become itself a "status of culture" where a label is more important than warmth, durability, and reflective coolness. The coolness is the label on the inside or more recently the outside.

How can we humble ourselves to stop this excessive consumption? We must somehow seek humbleness or eventually be forced with the destruction of the natural world that supports us that makes us genuinely happy. Two words that are similar in syntax: "humbleness" and "happiness", both ironically roll off the tongue with the same quiescence. The fact that the natural world can bring happiness and humble us is important in the realization to reduce consumption. It is again ironic that the word humbleness has an origin in the word "humus" another name for "soil", which is also an acronym for "earth".

To humble self and again be connected to the earth can be fulfilling. Producing food, clothing, and shelter from our own hands can be rewarding. Simply picking berries in the wild for a pie can be just as rewarding as tending your own garden as you experience the intricacies of nature. Choosing building products that you know the history of where it comes from whether it is a private woods or state/ national forest creates in the mind a connection to the earth. Wood for heating, cut and gathered from your local woods is a direct source of shelter heat without extraction from deep in the earth at great distances. To buy clothing, linens, and rugs, made by local artists or needle craftsmen whose source of material is from local farms creates appreciation for local land use. This avoids the use of huge container ships that consume vast amounts of fuel and release vast amounts of carbon for each trip abroad. This is true humbleness, where through our conscious we identify with "out of control" consumerism. We also come to realize that our happiness comes with a sense of place where simple things and their sources are close by.

The peace provided by nature is all around us now. Take a walk in the park, woods, or meadow. Soon an undisturbed state of mind will set in ... free from the mental conflicts of the fast-paced modern world. Visit the country and sample its splendor and simplicity.

This is man's place where ones past comes to life. Land humbles a person and if could speak would say " if you continue to destroy me by incessantly overstepping my ability to give back, I will humble you and bring you sadness, not happiness".

Hidden Realities

Our scientific world investigates and reacts to occurrences of man. When will it learn that what it needs to do is question and react to events of nature? One can study the events of a single organism to death, and then when it is dead what do you have left to solve? So, goes for the single human investigator of our natural world.

In this economic world we chase pest of field and forest as predators or competitors of our food and shelter. We do not consume the corn borer or gypsy moth; we just feel the need to stop the disturbances that are results of what eons of living have given them to survive.

For an example, the scientific world abounds with school children and scientists with great interest in the insect world. Each interest, in the evolution of such things, begins with squashing the creepy critter with the nearest object at hand, whether it be a fly swatter or insecticide. Gradually, after the insect keeps reappearing despite efforts that range from getting a bucket of water for the ant hill to spending a billion dollars on a chemical spraying program, we begin to think there is a larger picture. But the answer was in the garden hose and not the technology and economics of spraying.

For the garden hose carries moisture in the form of water. Water is fluid unless it is ice or vapor. If you could think like an insect these two forms of water are your downfall. Freezing and humidity (that create certain fungus) are your limiting environments. For an example, if we look at our history with the gypsy moth, drought and climatic patterns coincide with the spread and containment; Patterns of ecological disturbances followed by patterns of insect infestations. The world does not rotate around man's needs but around a cycle of disturbance until the disturbance changes the world, forever. Forever is in our time, not God's time.

We have created and studied wilderness since the 1940s as we realized that wilderness is the path of nature that is a model of sustainability. But have we come to understand it or tried to understand it with a reverence towards restoration of our disturbances? Funding of time scale applications of restoration that last decades cannot be in the hands of the government or universities but must be in the hands of a knowledgeable landowner. A landowner that knows the needs of its wildlife and the needs of the plants that support it. A caretaker is one that recognizes the changes in the soil as well as physical changes of light and temperature effects on the living organisms of it. One can pass this understanding to the next generation of caretakers who can add to this knowledge and teach his neighbors the same. How long before we recognize the reality that our survival as a species depends on this understanding?

Home Conservation

America is supposed to be a land of opportunity where one can have a sense of place. A location that supports you, one that gives you security of place as a landscape of peace through kinship & devotion. But it now has changed through too much opportunity and loss of place. It is changing to a land of competition and a place with no past. It is time to understand again what America is, but it will take humbleness and changes in the way we think.

In our wealth as a nation, we have created diverse lifestyles centered around the technology of modern tools of communication and travel. Clear sound, speed, and efficiency are all the parameters of this fast pace society. The simple, contemplating, and peaceful world needs to be found again. It needs to be found in our own backyard.

Most issues in conservation are driven by government, thus affected by budgets and the wielding of power. Laws can be made to protect things and create funds to develop conservation plans; but laws have no teeth and plans have no future without government employees being paid out of state or federal coffers or lead by administrators who have their own political agendas. For the good of all, government purchases land to be protected and then with the politics and pressures of multiple use we end up eventually over time destroying it. The burden on the individual or corporation to support this system through taxation only puts more pressure on the resources and removes man from the land further in his endeavors to support what he believes is conservation.

There is a move towards more local conservation, but is there a move to change the way that we perceive our home? A home is a place one finds peace and security for our family. But do we realize that we have disturbed or destroyed the home or habitat of other plants and animals to have our home?

Thirty years ago, natural resource laws required environmental review in the form of environmental impact statements and assessments on large and small projects that disrupted nature. Indeed, it has been just that -reviews of the problems of habitat destruction, little have they stopped human encroachment on the landscape. Is it time to develop a system that every human action must considers what was here prior?

The home is where we first realize our existence and visualize our surroundings. Should it not contain elements that imprint us to nature. Instead, we see home as a shelter from nature. It still can act as a shelter, but it must contain materials that connects us to the land from the very beginning. Is there reason that in nature, spring is the time when most creatures are born? These creatures are exposed to the sights and sounds of spring - this is the beginning when senses are tuned to these surrounding. Instinctual and behavior traits become alive at birth or shortly thereafter. It is these characteristics we must develop again in humans as first steps in connecting to the land. This is the beginning of a path towards becoming part of the land.

In these modern times, when urban communities dominate the population, exposure to nature at birth or even in a lifetime is a hard thing to come by. If we follow early life imprinting with an awareness of native habitat and home restoration ... perhaps in a few generations, we will make great strides in developing a reverence towards land that reflects true preservation.

Nature Out of Context

This is a day when words and phrases are being used out of context or used because they are a hot topic or buzz word to create images of their own meaning without respect for the original meaning. This is a sad day.

The word 'ecology" abuses would make Leopold turn over in his composting grave. The word ecology has been used is describing the economy, Wall Street, and social interaction structure. The only common thread of that the ecology of nature has with these is the fact all are facing catastrophes under the present actions of man. Until we take seriously understanding and preserving the physical, chemical, and biological interactions of all organisms that truly make this planet function the economic and social well-being of man will not continue.

The word "sustainability", which should always be connected to the true meaning of ecology, seems to be used to promote every product on the planet. The greatest rub is with "sustainable agriculture" is that corporate used as a buzz words so out of context to make a biased point that I cringed. An African American in a media blurb characterized the black man in America as an "endangered species". Maybe it would be better for the planet earth if all mankind were truly endangered ... we are approaching our limit of capacity quickly and this earth is reacting in violent ways. Perhaps, a sad situation can be cured by all races of man facing the ills of Planet Earth with actions that can make all humankind smile.

Intellectual Maturing of Man

Is there a process in which the importance of the wholeness of life and the time-tested ecosystems of Earth can be simply presented to the scientific communities, the political wills of the world, and the economic driving forces for their understanding and action? Can we create respect for this planet earth so that the entire human race can see this earth as complete and self-renewing and is essential for its own survival? I hope it is not too late for this process to succeed.

I believe the process must be universal in aspect and scope. It must be driven by ethics not laws. It must be excepted as a way of life and fulfillment of local culture. It must be an educational process that starts with the young and held in one's heart and mind into old age.

It will be based on our knowledge of all living things we presently recognize. It will contain the understanding of what it takes for all living things to survive through time and if they are to perish through this same time, we will know why and not have a hand in its demise. Diseases and pathogens will be limited by the wholeness of life and life's ability to resist their effects through land health. This process needs to create great changes in the scientific, business, and governmental systems. All need to be humbled by the prospect that if we do not change our systems many living things including man will die a horrible death. Human's greed, vanities, and jealousies on both the social and economic orders must recognize the importance of other species to be as great as humanity.

This process will take the knowledge of the relationship of all living things to making ethical acceptable decisions. It will move man towards a peaceful existence based on cooperation and harmony creating many cooperative communities that are locally self-serving for food, water and shelter. The natural resources of a community will be maintained and restored as well as understood by those that understand its past, grew up in it, and by those new members who enter it. Travel experiences between communities will take the knowledge and wisdom of local communities to a common world understanding of other self-renewing relationships between all. This common bond will carry the earth into sustainability. Scientific, political, and economic thinking and actions needs to shift towards the ecological, which Aldo Leopold coined as 'economically expedient' ... the trifecta of his famous quote "Examine each question in terms of what is ethically and esthetically right, as well as what is economically expedient. A thing is right when it tends to preserve the integrity, stability, and beauty of the biotic community, it is wrong when it tends otherwise".

Inventory of Life on Earth

We need to understand EO Wilson's writing of *Half-Earth, Our Planet's Fight for Life.* He speaks of humans needing a goal to save the earth species before species extinction accelerates beyond recovery. We do not have much time, he stated taxonomic descriptions of new species can take a decade or more. I say we need an immediate inventory of each seven million species we know of to understand their interconnectedness to their communities and methods for every human in that community to add to, understand, and act on making sure they survive. Newly discovered and ecologically described species can be added to this data base as it is refined to give more clues to our dependence on its existence.

If one specie becomes extinct in an ecosystem it enviably leads to the extinction of other species that were dependent upon the first extinct species ... for example, as providers of food or protection against predators. Yet, the effects to the physical, chemical, and biological worlds are even greater, putting even more survival pressure on other species and ecosystems.

This cascading effect can be witnessed on the effects of dams on river systems in Wisconsin or elsewhere. A dam collects silt and organic matter that has come from surrounding uplands into the flowage behind it.

The nutrients in this organic matter are more than the nutrients that would collect if it had the normal hydrology of a riverine system. Over time these nutrients create more aquatic growth, both on the bottom and suspended in the water column. Microscopic bacteria, aquatic plants, invertebrates, fish, reptiles, and aquatic mammals, all increase and do well until the nutrients accumulate to an excess, oxygen is depleted, and loss of species begins.

Eventually this accumulation of nutrients decreases oxygen levels so important to healthy aquatic life and species began to disappear and more resilient and tolerant species replace the original diversity. Among the first changes are the primary producers, phytoplankton, the free-floating aquatic plants of the water column. There increased abundance decreases the amount of light in the water column which in return decreases the photosynthetic light reaching the plants on the bottom and further limits the ability of fish and other species that depend on sight in capture of their food prey. Soon there is a species shift in the phytoplankton to species that cannot provide food for zooplankton and post larval fish. These species called blue green algae, are really a bacterial throwback to the early oceans, called cyanobacteria, that accumulated toxins that are lethal to many organisms, including young mammals, (i.e., humans and dogs).

A control of the phytoplankton and bacteria in a healthy riverine ecosystem is a myriad of clam species capable of filtering large amounts of plankton nutrients into food for aquatic fish and mammals, including otters. These clams (mollusks) are the first species to become endangered for at least three reasons: the toxic effects of the blue green algae (cyanobacteria), the increase silt load through its filtering food gathering "gills" inefficiencies, and the reduced recruitment and reproduction related to the presence of the dam.

In the life cycle of many clams, their reproducing larva are released to the water and attach to the gills of different species of fish. For example, the endangered Higgin's Eye Clam attaching to the gills of walleye, and sauger. These fish species require high quality water with plenty of oxygen and migrate each spring to rubble gravel areas to spawn... and can stack below dams in their effort to follow the water. Behind these dams, where enough silt and organic matter accumulate low oxygen under the ice or during summer heavy phytoplankton blooms can kill or stress these species. Normally, the clam larval fall from the fish gills and establish new colonies of filtering clams.

These clam colonies have especially become abundant below the dams where walleye migration upstream is limited, and oxygen is abundant.

The ecological connections of a riverine system interrupted for a century or more by dams and nutrients from the agriculture and industry in the watershed can eventually lead to extinction of the flora, fauna, and microscopic organisms that make it all function. It is our ecological understanding of the specifics of ecosystem functioning that can be used address any disturbances to pristine natural reserves that still exist on this planet earth or to meticulously restore disturbed ecosystems.

Land Possession

Land as opposed to property is something not bought and sold. Land is an area that is a home to a combination of soil, water, plants, and animals no matter who is in possession. It is the understanding of life on the land and an ethic that follows that makes it a cherished possession.

I once met a wise forester that saw more than the cellulose of trees but saw the forest as a community. He was unable to take our young biologist group to see what he sees in the field, but he did the best he could by showing us a slide presentation of photographic memories accompanied by a zealous presentation. What I saw inspired me to go up to him at the end of this presentation to ask, "What can I do to save the land?" His response was "One should go out and buy a 40, 80, or 160 acres of land, whatever land one could afford, understand everything on that land, and protect it with your life".

After graduation I began work as a field biologist and every location I worked, I had my eyes open for property that I could possibly afford. But moving from area to area and position to position the time never came for purchase and rightly so. I was looking for property, not land! My eyes were indeed looking but not seeing. I knew so little about the land, but I did have the penchant to learn as much as I could and the opportunity to work in a variety of natural resource management fields that provided knowledge.

But I never forgot what the aging forester said. I also knew that this forester, and others that I was exposed to, were students of Aldo Leopold. Aldo's way of teaching was not to tell you anything direct but to give enough information so your reasoning abilities will prevail with the answer- and better yet left you with a long-lasting impression.

Eventually, I was able to give my own presentations and this wise forester's words were pondered further. The land does have dimensions, but they were not important if you are not capable of perceiving it. It could have ownership, but it was not necessary for possession ... what was important was the understanding of it.

This understanding means to ecologically comprehend the connection between soil, water, plants, and animals. It means to understand how geological processes, climate, and weather have shaped the land. It means to comprehend how plants have built the soil and how this long-term relationship created conditions for animals-including us- for survival on this land.

The resulting intellect and reasoning ability will allow humanity to make proper choices about the land. If humans are good enough at gaining this understanding, the ability of the land to sustain itself and homo sapiens will be perpetual. The need to "protect it with your life "at that time will not seem like a sacrificing matter as the protection of the land will come naturally.

This forester's quote appears to most as a philosophical parable or idealism at its utopian peak. Yet the message is basic and clear for all to gain hold of. It creates an attitude and goals that are perpetual and youthful. It implies that there is always something to learn and with this knowledge comes an understanding for a lasting relationship with life and land. It brings self-preservation to the land and man.

The significance of this quote is it has no geographic or temporal limits. It can be applied to a planet, a continent, a country, or state but more important it can be applied to your own back yard. It develops a discipline and ethic that can be touched and felt locally and an attitude that can be universally applied. It has no age limit but is best created in youth. When created at a young age this knowledge of the land will both protect it and sustain all. By the time this youth matures a wisdom and land ethic will be created to pass on to their children and grandchildren.

Land Bouts

This competitive age in America has brought a sense of urgency to life but at the same time a separation from it. Today's popularity of prize fighting, pro wrestling, pro football, and the glamour of beauty are examples of this lifestyle - you only have so much time that you can hold the edge and make a scene. These diversions, paces, and perspectives have temporal limits. This place that man has placed himself in is not Eden or the heavens of mythology, it is only an earth that has limitations and problems. Man is not at the center of this earth but only an organism that has a function and a limit. If we do not give earth the attention and understanding it needs the problems will soon limit man's presence and his ability to make a difference.

Sociologists have recognized that the genetic foundation of human nature has created a modern man that is persistently injurious and ill-adapted to meet the decisions that must be made to protect the earth. In the environmental field actions made for protection can create quick hostility towards a newcomer or a competing group that may have innovative ways to approach problems. Therefore, the status quo is maintained by the political arena that surrounds the world of conservation and environmental conditions.

As more people occupy an area the competition increases, and politics replaces ethics in the decision-making process. Decisions are less localized as the knowledge to solve environmental problems are too much for local expertise. The protection of the environment for the good of all by government becomes compromises for the good of a few greedy competitors able to manipulate the political system through government legalities and wordsmithing the law to alter the original intent.

If we had the time... or would take the time ... to understand this situation, we would find that a majority people would make choices that are good for the environment. But the action to initiate this choice is hindered by a competitive world. In this country the choices are also hindered by a high standard of living that few are willing to sacrifice. "Living one day at a time" means life is complex and busy but I want it to be simple. In poor countries "one day at a time" means that this day may be your last and the competitive world leaves little room for philosophy.

Take the situation away from the individual and family you find those with authority and power are not interested in the long-term welfare of all - especially as it pertains to the environment. Our leaders fall to the wants of corporate greed. Resource exploitation without the long-term consequences on a local community is often the result. The individual's base instinct for freedom of choice naturally wants to limit laws leaving the protection of the resource today to the bottom line of corporate profits and ability of lawyers and lobbyist to do minimum for the environment.

An ethical view towards the resource might be to utilize the resource making a minimum impact on the environment and at the same time restoring other related resources in the same ecosystem. If this became common practice the local opposition based on "not in my backyard" might be a thing of the past. Unless the community is educated on how they affect what their backyard's ecosystem and what is needed to restore it, the opposition of use of the resource can always be fed by the emotional values of distrust of what it does not understand. This prolongs the security of maintaining the status quo.

Eventually the land bouts become larger as more land is destroyed and individual freedoms become more restricted. The borders of a country as well as neighborhood fences become battle grounds of emotion for what is mine. Selfishness will continue until man and child understand that they may not only be an individual in humanity but are also the brain box for the fate of larger ecosystems. Like a boxer, the environment will be finished when it is punched in the head enough that the brain no longer functions.

Land Conservation Delays

The benefits of conservation practices and restoration are often held back by the agencies whose missions are clearly responsible for our natural resources. We have created the system that Aldo Leopold visional statement predicted " When will government conservation become like a mastodon and be hampered by its own dimensions". Size is relative to a complexity that instead of giving relative input to a conservation problem creates channels of delay.

These channels of delay come in many forms. A good idea is stalled or stifled simply by the power of an upper-level position that does not have the feeling for the land and does not fully understand the specific management problem or restoration situation. It is often a matter of budget, therefore if it is not funded it is often forgotten, unless the person in the field is passionate enough to find local conservation groups who are also inspired to keep the project moving. Even these local groups are limited in their ability to raise money and now more than ever are tied to state or national conservation group who has their own mastodon encumbrances.

Often the connection of the restoration or conservation practice is indirect but ecologically connected to the resource problem and another resource agency is responsible. The agriculture practices that have severe impact on water quality are an example where two different agencies have been involved for decades with truly little improvement in water quality and soil loss.

We go on changing and creating laws; recreating operating codes and procedures; and selectively enforcing and implementing them, while the original mission to preserve and protect are forgotten and the resources continue to degrade. We are so busy creating systems to protect or restore resources we do not realize the changes in the ecosystem have occurred and many parts of the regulatory systems are no longer needed. Yet policy does not react to this; time and money continues to be wasted.

Our own successes in restoration may eliminate a need for long standing functions. Our goal of restoration should always be to create a self-sustaining system. For an example, does one still need fish hatcheries or animal rearing facilities when restoration of habitat creates self-reproducing populations? Does growth in a conservation organization parallel success in its conservation mission or create a complexity that hampers or delays action.

Land Restoration

What is land restoration? It is one's realization that man has changed the natural world, not for the better, and in return wishes to right the wrong created by progress. These wrongs were probably often unknown to man in his quest for ... at first for survival and then for wealth. Changing of the landscape first began in gathering wood for a fire and has not ended yet in his forever search for fuel to drive his machines and build his luxuries.

The first step in land restoration is to admit that one owes the natural world an apology and wants to make things right again. This comes with a commitment; whether it be in a national energy policy that gives back to the atmosphere or in the backyard where planting native plants for insects, fur, and feather.

The second step is to lead our children to understanding our need to correct the wrongs we have wrought on the land. An understanding that says that everything we take for granted everyday – the food we eat, the clothes we wear, and the power that runs our lights and computers – comes at a cost to nature and the land. One must teach these fundamental connections early so there thought processes are tuned to make changes in their consumptive ways; but also, to correct the degraded changes we have brought to this earth. They must learn to not except the common species that are out our back door and that are common because our construction of buildings and roads have created a near monoculture from the diversity of life that once was here before human abundance. We are responsible in restoring this diversity.

The third step is to simply restore. An inventory of the present landscape and an extensive plan seems to be the norm of active re-creation, but time is not on our side. Do not spend much time and energy on these activities but make moves and actions based on the observations of the connections between fauna and flora and how past and present human actions have affected them; then make decisions and actions that increases the original native species and diversity that were present before our disturbances. Our initial actions may not be altogether successful, but further observations of how the restoration species react to our conscious attempts at restoration will make the next attempt more successful as diversity is slowly restored. Does the planting of wildflowers attract new insects to the bloom? Are these blooms and insects consumed by more varieties of insects and birds? And does a decaying flower renew the life of the soil and the land? These are simple questions to simple actions and reactions!

To change man from being a destructive consumer may be caused by a desperate world that can no longer provide clean air, food, or water. This desperation should not create wars or laws to claim a right to these things but create a conscious mind that thinks we can change what we have wrought.

Lazy Cultural Threats

Nobody walks far anymore, maybe a few do, but darn few. Most of us walk from the house to the motor vehicle in the garage, from the couch to the refrigerator, from the laundry to the kitchen or bedroom. The more ambitious may have an exercise machine that views the morning news and weather from a video screen in front of them. Fewer still venture outside, solely concerned with health fitness of heart, lungs, and body. While exercise is important to the poor human condition in the United States, most fail to walk and see nature in the world around us.

We have come to expect that things need to come to us rather than we going to it — which is mostly nature at its best or worst as the world heats up. No wonder many doubt global warming as our cultural life today is removed from the effects of its causes. Or maybe not.

How do we deal with the heat that is forecast for this summer day? We make sure, the air conditioner is turned on and plan our activities, so we are not in the heat. Or if we want to be active, we take our high horsepower boat or automobile with air conditioning, to the lake or river to find a place to go fast so the air cools us; often the water itself is too polluted to enter so a swim in the waterways of nature to cool us is out of the question. We have the option to take the kids to the swimming pool or let them sit in the cool of the house watching or playing videos. All involve an artificial experience or a technical – based power experience.

So, what do we do to change? We walk out our back door …and change will occur. The change can occur by observing the growth of a plant that occurs from day to day. Ask a gardener. On your hands and knees in a cultivated patch you can observe a lot. If you get on your feet and expand your vision with walking you will experience even more. You will see a landscape filled with urban developed and intense agriculture areas dominated by plants that do not belong there. You will not notice this at first, but you will notice that a few bright colors or shapes of plants dominate your visual horizon of your walk.

It is natural for the mind once focused on an object to ask what it is and want a definition that describes it. A search online or at the library can tell you what it is. The description you find will most likely be that this plant is an exotic or invasive plant that is plentiful on a disturbed habitat. If one investigates further there are environmental education efforts to create awareness and make efforts to stop the spread of these species, yet the effort and widespread understanding that their presence is caused by "habitat destruction" is left as that.

So, what exactly is "habitat destruction? If you continue with your walk and keep asking questions of what you see, you may find remnant native plants trying to hold on despite "habitat destruction". If you do not give up on your walk because it is too much effort you are at risk of making it a habit. With this habit and extra endorphins entering your brain you will increase your curiosity enough to ask why these invasive are doing so well and the native remnant flower is not.

Is it just a matter of population? Of course! But why? Does the timing of mowing by the town, city, and county road crews favor the growth of exotics and weed species over native plants? Could it be the compaction of the soil? Or the disturbance in building and maintaining the road or the planting and maintaining of crops adjacent limit the survival of native seeds that often germinate within an inch of the surface? Maybe that native remnant plant is dependent upon a "companion plant" that can add just the right amount of nitrogen or some other substance to the soil for it to grow and produce seed. But of course, we resist any change that even comes with awareness and continue to only recognize the many cultivated plants of our lawns, gardens or agricultural fields … any other plant is a still a weed.

Soon, I hope you will walk away from the television, computer, refrigerator, and washer/dryer and start a conversation of what habitat destruction is. The energy to run these appliances must come from someplace. The electric grid power lines also cleared native habitat beneath by spraying and cutting right-a-ways without considering the same effects? Of course, these power line grids that provide much of this energy runs on coal and shale oil that also creates widespread habitat destruction. On a more positive thought, can our modern initiatives into solar and wind power facilities be coupled with an ethic to restore the land around them to native plant communities?

These are times for change. Our children can learn more by taking an interest in the natural world as our genetic code does not let us forget where we came from. If natural habitat continues to give away to development and intense agriculture how will our human genetic makeup react? Maybe our own legs will shorten or become useless, our eyes will dim from color and shapes, or maybe there will be nothing left to think about on a walk through the city landscape or solid rows of crops.

Making World Connections

The world is full of scientist who are specialist in one field or another. Their discipline and expertise have been developed through towered universities and research specific to a problem or cause. For decades to centuries these individuals have gathered in meetings, seminars, and symposiums to share their worlds. It is time that the plethora of expertise be connected for a common purpose ... to save our ecosystems and thus our Planet Earth from themselves and others.

The two primary obligations of science have always been discovery and communication. No single science can give a balanced aspect of the elemental world of nature to our modern citizen. We need an expansive scale and collection of scientific knowledge presented to the public, government officials, engineers, and businessmen to create long lasting ecological and economic benefits rather than the immediate returns we expect in today's modern societies.

The world economy and communication networks have become global. It is time that the knowledge of our natural world be collected and utilized to create a data base to assess the effects that the world economy is having on the biosphere. We can use these communication networks to gather the science information created over the centuries and store it in computers with mega analysis capabilities. The movement of digitizing past and present scientific knowledge has been part of this communication revolution, but it is time to put this data in a form to use in solving the world-wide ecological problems. This is the first step.

The second step is to use this new data base and create an education system that is based on man's relation to nature itself. An education system at the elementary, to primary, to secondary levels that is adeptly designed to simply communicate the connectiveness of the earth and its inhabitants. The purpose is to create a pattern of civilizing evolution in which the concept of ecology will play a major part in developing political and economic support for true ecological restoration. This will eventually create an atmosphere of global citizens that are aware.

The worlds of biology, chemistry, and physics will come together as the inventories of what we know about plants and animals and their relationship to each of these fields is amassed in a mega data base. This relationship is where the true ecological connections will be made, and a clear picture of our world resources will be visible for the first time. There should be no filter on this data collection that limits purpose or collapses its broad scope. This is as important, for the result will create the broadest understanding of our limited resources and a future security for survival.

Separateness

Modern culture has physically removed us from the land. In our digital computer culture, we are being programed into thinking that reality is only a mental process. These two acts of civilization have taken us from viewing the land as a living organism to viewing the land as a mechanism. When did this process begin? Did it begin when we ran out of raw wilderness in our western movement? Or did it begin with the creation of science that in its speed towards knowledge ignored the philosophical question "Why"?

We have created a competitive society that is based on advancing oneself beyond that of another ... to get someplace quicker and be smarter at doing it than the next person. All things must be viewed objectively, unknowns calculated, amounts quantified, and disposable raw material changed for our use. This is the mode that we have created in this modern world. With this quest for progress, we have lost the strength to identify that the real power lies not in the human realm but in the spirit of natural world we are constantly trying to alter.

We have approached conservation of our natural resources in the same manner. We have looked these resources as raw material to be preserved. We must identify what they are, count how much we have, and make sure we utilize them wisely. We created Latin names, collected a few items from the field, and then carried them to a lab to inspect through our created scientific methods. This sense of identification and collection led to experimentation with management. Additionally, as time passed, humans felt more secure and comfortable in the office, lab, or classroom than out in the field. We create students that can identify, collect, and experiment out of a lab manual or photographic guide with preserved specimens in hand. We were on our way to removing ourselves from the land and becoming virtual.

With the digital age of video and computers the hold that classrooms and labs have on an urban society have increased even more. Technical digital producers can show details of the wild from the courtship of the largest predator to the life in a drop of pond water and bring them to the labs and classrooms. In time these actions will not create a picture of where we fit in the natural world- but that we do not fit in at all - but are separate from it; we are above nature, observing with a remote camera, and not part of the picture.

With our disconnection with the land, we have progressed to the point where we have unconsciously lost the meaning of words. The words "common sense" originally meant "other faculty (of humans) that supposedly united and interpreted impressions of the five senses". Without full uses of our senses, we now use the words "logic" and "judgment" as it pertains to the thought process not our sensory perceptions. We have come to a point where sensory experiment and observation are no longer important in the decision-making process as scientific principals are driving the logic of society. Along with this instinct loss has come the loss of reverence towards the land.

What deep strivings move us towards the land? The answer: our senses developed during our evolution in nature. If we look back at childhood memories, there is always a sentimental moment we can remember. Most often this moment is tied to something from the natural world. A single camping, canoeing, hiking, or fishing trip can be the most precious occasion in our lives. The closeness of a wild animal - a fish, a deer, or a small insect can be a poignant instant to remember forever. What does it take to transfer these cherished occasions of our past into a devotion to the natural world around us? We can expand our horizons by using our senses again to see nature's beauty. With this feeling will come an understanding. With this understanding will come a vital attainment that there is more to understand ... and much is being lost!

When the mechanized world is overwhelming, we turn to the natural world for peace. Why cannot we return something to this world for what it has provided us. Can we continue to plunder nature without recourse? It is easy to blame disasters of weather on nature and even easier to tangle manmade causes with the weather. What is difficult to admit is that we have not made decisions by considering the ecological consequences. We build, farm, consume, waste, and recreate without a thought towards long term effects. We live our lives without considering the hereafter on our home, Planet Earth.

We need to take time for a spiritual awareness of the land. Every time we view a bird in the bird feeder during winter or a video of a time-lapsed plant developing in the spring we must say to ourselves this is only a reminder that we must walk out the door. If we fail to see the natural world directly, when we walk a short distance from our shelter, we should then be aware of the significance of them not being there. One upshot is that there is something drastically wrong with the technological world and there is something missing in your life. You are now asking the question "Why…?"

Taking for Granted

Until early this fall morning it had not rained here for a month. This is unusual for September and October in Wisconsin, just as uncommon as the record amount of rain we received in our normally dry months of this summer. Most of us are aware that it all balances out as average rain fall. Most of us do not realize there is cycle to this annual rain average; over a 11-year period from wet to dry to wet again. This cycle has been recorded in Wisconsin for over a century. This is weather as we know it, yet signs of climate change are all around us.

Climate change, being slow in progress by our immediate perspectives of today, is hidden in the statistics of averages and in the conflicts of scientific debate and doubt; but is showing up with the slowly stressed and dying maples on the street corner. We take weather, our modern way of life, and the unnatural world around us in stride with our heads in the sand ... no concrete.

Climate experts have predicted that with global warming certain species of trees will be lost from Wisconsin. Sugar maple forest trees beyond 2025 will leave Wisconsin and only be found north into Canada. A tree does not suddenly just die or disappear from an area of growth and survival. The death is slowly affected by the stresses of too hot a temperature in summer and changes in moisture levels. Maple trees – especially hard maples - are showing stress more than soft maples that are found along our river systems.

How is one to react to these slow changes in our climate? Is it clear that this has happened before, and certain species have adapted or perished? We must adapt too. If we look to the plant communities that were here in pre-settlement times - less than two hundred years ago - you will find species that will do well in these times. The oaks/hickory tree species and the prairie plants of the oak savanna and tall grass prairie ecosystems are local examples how native species, that are genetically tuned to withstand drought and harsh conditions survived. But do not believe that climate change only effect on these species; humans have eliminated these plant communities already with the plow and bulldozer.

The Beat of Life's Drum

Why cannot people view the land and associated plants and animals as part of their community? Do these occupants of the land have an obligation to members of the Chamber of Commerce? Have they not already pay dues to commerce with their lives? If we could only vision and understand the intricacies of the biological community that supports us!

Since of creation of central park in New York, Americans have been obsessed with the green lawns, cement, and landscaping that plague our country today. These artificial buffers of our homes and communities have removed us from the natural world not only esthetically but ethically. Leopold said "We can only love things that we can see, touch, and feel ..." Over time this separation from nature by buffers of green lawn and pavement have made nuisances of anything wild entering this space.

We long for vacations in remote areas to get away from the mundane and artificial world we have created. We seek the wild areas of the forest to view large mammals such as deer and bear. But even on arrival to this area we choose to view them at a petting zoo or at our favorite restaurant feeder. At the same time, we long for a retirement home on a pristine lake or a tropical island; yet we require an 18-hole golf course next to each as we could not do without the short grass in our departure paradise. We continuously seek a change from what we are exposed to everyday, but when we find this diversion, we seek the security of the routine we are trying to escape!

In the next few generations, we will continue to condition ourselves to expanding this manmade environment and soon all undisturbed areas will be islands. Our children will enter the digital world of the virtual and wildlife will be closer on videos and the Discovery Channel but farther from our conscious mind.

This anthropocentric conditioning has also driven our leaders in natural resource management and environmental protection.

Most activities in conservation are directed towards improvement of human-centered effects on the environment. This is appropriate to protect our water and air quality, recreational interest, and not often enough the aesthetic of the natural environment. Ventures to repair of terrestrial and aquatic habitats is expensive and we make efforts mainly through human and corporate guilt financed non-profits.

The ecosystem management approach to land care is still in its infancy. Loss and degradation of terrestrial and aquatic ecosystems grossly exceed recovery and repair, bringing ecosystem collapses that our society fails to recognize. These diminished ecosystem functions will eventually reduce the economic sustainability of our environment unless we can adjust our education system and land management to correct our approach.

In Wisconsin, since the 1930's, there has been a requirement that environmental education be a part of the curriculum. In schools, the short time of our classroom periods and expense of transportation to the outdoors do not allow the student to be exposed to observing nature directly. The ethic towards the natural world cannot develop without a child using his instincts of sight, touch, and smell. If there is to be a feeling or motivation to protect and restore the natural world this standard classroom approach must change to place children nearer to nature. The new trend in education towards block periods in secondary education hopefully will eventually reach the primary school level where class time allows hands on activities in nature to be used to understand the fundamentals of reading, writing, and reasoning skills.

There is a centering in environmental education on pollution and recycling that concentrates on the local action. Does it connect pollution and recycling to the natural world? Does it communicate what habitat and ecosystem exists where an open pit bauxite (aluminum) mines are created? Does it explain the operation of the mine or uses and restoration of these mines after this mineral has been extracted? Does it understand the fossil fuels that are burned in the recycling effort of transportation and creation of the new soda can or plastic bottle?

How does this relate to pollution and the economy? The most important question is "does this environmental education gives our youth a perspective of how we can preserve and restore the natural world?" A simple curriculum that includes leading a student through a single industrial process of a local industry and ties it to a local habitat can create an awareness that can be carried into adulthood action and decisions.

Today's question is " Does man have the capabilities to understand the habitat that once existed where he lives and the ability to restore it while still maintaining an economic viability that supports him and the ecosystem?" For example, soil and climate determine what natural plant and animal species can exist on the land. It also determines the success of domestic plant and animal culture that can be sustained. This interaction of the natural and domestic world and how we understand and deal with the conflicts between them will lead to the success of both worlds.

We must understand that these worlds are separate entities that have merits of their own. But it is the natural world that created the stabilities and efficiencies that sustains life. This very fact is justification for the preservation and restoration of it. Restoration is one method by which we will come to understand the natural world. It will give us the knowledge to sustain our own economy that will be compatible with the natural world.

The Collision Course

The view of the land we see from the hilltop today is not what it was yesterday. It has changed from a wild scene to a pastoral landscape; to a disrupted one. Our ability to perceive what has happen to the land is hidden by the rose-tinted glasses of the scientific world of progress and production.

Before human civilization native plant succession on a landscape progressed from a grassy habitat to a closed canopy of trees through natural succession. Human culture has created several other journeys for the landscape. In the American Midwest, the new successional route is from the pre-settlement prairies of native grasses; to a pasture of exotic grasses, to a corn field, to a shopping mall; another from native grass to a subdivision; and still another from native grass to an industrial complex. These are routes of progress and production that drive the economic landscape of Wall Street. Yet all these paths of production can be traced to their origin in the undisturbed wild habitat. How long will it take before this economic productivity ends because these original natural scenes no longer exist?

Food, shelter, and water are the basics for survival of all organisms from the producers to the consumers, to the decomposers. Food and shelter are provided to us, the consumer, by the primary producers - the plants. Water is shared with all organisms; it is the carrier of the nutrients to all living things. When will these basics of all life no longer provide for any of us?

Maintaining the integrity of the soil to produce food and fiber for our existence will continue to be essential for our survival. Agriculture in America today focuses on pure stands of grain dependent upon an exact formula of fertilization and genetics to meet geographic and maximum growth conditions. The condition of the soil is manipulated to meet the conditions of the crop. Farmers insist we need to use these practices to feed the poor halfway around the world. They are without a pocketbook and may have thin or no soil on a hillside they are about to lose from erosion from the removal of trees & brush for food and shelter. These same families are they need economic development to increase their standard of living and create income to buy our grain products. Where in this picture do you see the maintaining of integrity of our soil? What will happen as temperature and rainfall shifts as a part of climate change reduce the production of our most fertile soils?

Agriculture understands the value of crop rotation in building nitrogen and knowing what to add to make a specific crop grow. It also knows what pesticide to add to stop the invasion of exotics that do well on disturbed ground or in a monoculture environment. It does this with justification that agriculture needs to feed the world and its own economics. Yet the plants and animals that made the soil that grew the crop slowly disappears from the landscape. About the time we realize that our soil can no longer support more and more production we will realize the value of what we have lost from the natural landscape.

At what point will we realize that the economy of the world is based on maintaining the ecology of a small area in which we live? Populations of humans explode because we have the strong desire to make our own personal genetic code survive. At the lowest standard of living, it is our local environment we first destroy to feed and clothe our family. As one's standard of living increases from survival to luxury, we affect larger and larger areas consuming more and more resources.

Our understanding of how mankind effects the natural world is clouded by the vast number of ways we effect it and our preponderance to not let things close to us unless we understand it or can control it.

We demand scientific facts and studies but also reserve the prerogative to ignore the results for its biases. The complexes of an ecosystem cannot be researched economically but must be understood with empirical obedience. Ecosystems, besides being complex, are also not static and are continually evolving. They can cloud the results of scientific study because of variations in time, place, and conditions.

If we approach life science education with a penchant for observation and hands-on experimentation on the land, we can again create a land society that can replenish what we have lost. With this ecological education will come an ability to create new products from the land that will support both the land that it comes from and man's needs. A knowledgeable private and public team with these tools and a land ethic can lead to both ecological restoration and preservation.

Our present policies in preservation conservation of buying land and protecting those lands already set aside may not work in the long run to save Planet Earth. Our present population, land use, and lifestyles have destroyed biodiversity. Cultural economic uses and future multiple use of the land will not maintain any biological integrity that remains if we stay on our present course. But a land society that understands ecological mechanisms and applies modern agricultural knowledge will lead to sustainable sustenance on the local landscape.

The efficiencies of energy transfer of nutrients from the soil to man will increase. But most important of all ... humans will realize what they need to survive is the same as what all other organisms need.

The Flow

There is a flow of energy that passes through all life that man expounds through the disciplines of the thinking mind. This energy is universal, and one would expect thinking man to eventually understand the ramifications of this energy flow and move to preserve and expand this flow for the benefit of all; but he has not yet. We can only hope that he does.

One aspect of physical science dwells on energy for human use. It takes energy from beneath the earth in the form of minerals and gases and transfers it into fuels to operate our autos, heat our homes, and run our factories. These factories in return take these earth-sourced minerals and gases and turn them into products we use and consume. We have been successful at this exploitation. Technology drives this feat of man's knowledge to new heights every year. The energy of the imagination becomes the ideas that create new or improved uses of our original earth-bound resources.

These resources are not universally distributed over this planet so through trade and transportation this energy creates wealth— an energy that by another definition becomes power. Power is not true energy but a form of greed if anything, a negative energy, or force. With this type of power, we have again, universally, separated the wealthy and the poor with both continuing to consume energy on different levels. The rich consume a vast array of products and waste even more. The poor use the basic energy found in the fuel of wood and waste to create a small fire to cook food and for warmth. This negative energy of greed now fuels wars over who has and who has not – rich or poor.

The energy flows of consumerism and war are taking a toll on this earth and a few are taking notice. These few are the thinking people that care, and a positive flow of eternal energy is emerging that hopefully will right the wills of the negative influence on this earth and its inhabitants before it is too late. Circling to the concept of physical energy, it is the sun, that all life depends on, that will reverse the influences of the earth extracted energy resources. Will enough people of this earth s face the sunshine and feel the warmth of what is important in life, look within for answers to the future, and not at the past where possessions were the maladies of any developing culture?

The happiest people I have known are humble beings that see pleasure in the natural world that they connect with by being part of it. They become children to the world around them by viewing every natural living and non-living thing with awe. Time is suspended during these quiet reflective times; care is given to the land by these working individuals … and returned for the benefit and flow of energy for all this world.

The Land Pursuit

The modern-day history of the preservation of our natural resources abounds with organizations, government bodies, and those individuals who were valiant heroes in each. Where is the uncommon hero of the landscape?

Our society is so busy that there is little time to self-reflect on personal needs that are also vital needs to all. We have become dependent upon professional staffs of conservation organizations to determine what we want conserved or how the resources will be used. As we dependent on their expertise we give them power to make decisions based on a narrow field of specialty and apply it to a contorted political process. Yet the public in general have come to distrust the magnitude of government conservation as now laws affect every aspect of our lives. Our personal needs are being controlled without a self-reflecting understanding of the land and how conservation policy and law now effects use.

The participation of the individual in nature and society is a need that must be elevated to community action. We must recognize that conservation of our resources is not a collection of data or a controlled inventory; but an exchange of thoughts and actions on how we can preserve the existence of nature. Today this process must be update from the action of preservation to an act of restoration because of the profound effect we have had on the land. We must paint ourselves back into the landscape and elevate our knowledge of it to wisdom.

Our present view of the land has been distorted by the uses we have developed for it; to grow crops, to motor through, to build houses on , etc. These uses have come with the speed of technology and often not with the slower speed of wisdom. To view the land with a history thousand times older than our lives is the first step in taking a personal reflection to its needs. Do you know the origin of the soil that your community has been placed on? Do you know the life history of the original plants and animals (including humans) that were on the land before you? Do you know what happened to the land that caused the disappearance of the native species?

But where are we today? Our foods and shelters are still tied to the land, but we are less aware of it. Modern cultures have become so disconnected to the land and have become dependent on the middleman. But even the producers- the loggers, farmers, or fishermen have removed themselves from the land by their enclosed, air conditioned, stereo filled cabs and need of technology to produce more for us. These producers have chosen the route of technology to meet a distant market for a distant person. How much satisfaction and understanding of the land could you get by getting to know this producer? Could you buy lumber from a local woodsman and travel through the countryside to pick it up? Could you travel to the lake, oceanside, or the local fish farmer to buy fish or the country market to buy produce? Simple pleasure comes with this simple start in returning to the land.

Hunting and gathering societies of the past, and those remaining today, have considered nature as their home and community. Knowledge of nature and its occupants is the essence of their life and religion to be passed on through the generations. The seasonal availability and utilization of the animals and plants was tied to every aspect of human society. From their clothes and shelter to their rituals and festivals early man's life and survival was tied to the land. There was purpose in this connection to the land. How can we restore this perception in our views of nature today?

Today land appears to be divided into private and public. A closer look finds these boundaries as one of perspective. As public land use changes there are activities of users that show less of a connection to the land. Just as technology pulls man away from the land, use of instruments of technology on public land will eventually destroy its place for quiet contemplation and the wonders of nature. Gadgets can be limited, use cannot, for the mere fact it is public. On private land we can limit both use and gadgets – but often not the ethic to stop the effects of technology; but once we recognize we do not own nature, its true value ... will be recognized and restored.

We need to take the remnant traditions that we have with the land today and expand them using our scientific society as a catalyst. We must show our children early in life that the landscape is important to our wellbeing; that the sunrise of early morning holds the songs of nature and that song is tied to the habitat that we can affect. We must develop vocations that focus on understanding the interrelatedness of the natural world ... and how to identify, protect, and restore these interconnections. We cannot affect public policy towards public land unless we understand early in life the principles of the simple and smaller world that surrounds us and take it to heart.

The Land Spell

There are few words in the English language that carry more definitions ... yet with vagueness ... than the word "Spell". As a verb it is word of taking children's minds from sounds and letters to communication. It is also a word verb used as a forecast of what is to come. As a noun it is word used to describe enchantment or fascination. Another meaning relates to a diverse foggy duration of time or release of duty in time. It is a word that can put our treatment of the land in perspective.

The land is not in static time, but our perspective of the land can be. Our view of the land often comes from our experiences with it over a short stay on the land. A child lost in the woods or having a near drowning experience in water will probably avoid each as his life progresses. Yet a child's week at camp, a visit to grandpa's farm, or a single fishing trip can be a spell that the land makes that can either grow into an understanding of it with more time ... or be a distant vagueness of a pleasant memory if not developed further.

To take a child, so full of questions, to hear the land in springtime is the first step in conservation education. It is the beginning of not only their abilities to communicate with the land but the beginning of the seasonal life cycle of growth. The importance of soil, atmosphere, and rain are never closer than during spring. The principles of chemistry, biology, and physical science are all within arm's reach when you are three feet tall ... even if you do not know how to spell. But nature can be the incentive instrument that hands-on education must use not only to develop the future skills of sustainable technology but the future skills of saving and restoring the land.

A visit from a family with small children on Sunday to an abandoned farm is an example of the open and not so carefree minds of children. The five-year-old picks up a rock at the edge of the field and looks at it curiously for a moment and then begins to stack them in a pile. As soon as the pile is only a few rocks, the child notices the large rocks that have been pushed from the field; over one hundred years ago they had been bulldozed over the steep bank towards the wetland so the field could be used for crops. When this was explained to the child the pile of five rocks and others were thrown further from the edge of the field with the help of her two-year-old brother. What is in store for the second visit? Explaining where the rocks came from that got on the field? Or explaining how the rocks are affecting the growth of the trees of the steep hillside.

The two-year-old I was told had a fascination with insects. On our walk the child noticed an inch-long western chorus frog which quickly disappeared from his reach. The child began to cry because he could not find and catch the frog. The parents caught a glimpse of the frog and finally found it. The frog was eventually captured and placed in a plastic apple bag. The return to the house placed the frog in shallow water container and a photo of the frog was produced from a book to both the two and five-year-old amazement. The first words in their preschool vocabulary had been spelled.

What is to come of our natural resources if our children do not grow up close to them? Will the demand for resources and technology push a political process where the value of the resource is only consumptive? Will growth of our urban areas continue to destroy habitat and promote multiple use of public conservation reserves severing any hope of preserving what is remaining? It up to us to create a spell on our children of genuine love and appreciation of nature that will carry into a social and economic movement that will lead to a harmony with it.

There is an unconscious fascination with the land. It is some primordial feeling that is stirred in all people. It takes on the need for possessive care of the land. It defends the land against all intruders whether it be man, beast, or pest. It creates a pride for land beauty and maintenance. These unrealized perspectives of the land at one time were carried from the country to the city. Here they were altered by generations of time to a false sense of what the land should be like. This hidden sensation has taken on an urban perspective with the dimensions and qualities of a city lot. On an attempt to reach out to the real land we are making decisions based on this new false sense.

This false sense has been evident in the development of sensitive areas. We insist on changing what is left of the natural world to create green space to counter the intense use of development. These green spaces are to provide a natural setting and an escape from the concrete world of roads and streets. For example, natural stream corridors that intersect the urban areas were the last refuges for nature. They were defined as floodplains and floodways in the name of economics and public protection. Rather than to conserve these areas and maintain their natural beauty we have broadened the definition of a park to meet our needs. The floodplain has been turned into ballparks and soccer fields, larger lawns of short grass, providing a manicured nutrient wash way that slowly destroys the stream corridors just by removing the buffer. And now we are progressing to narrow the buffer even more by creating paved pathways to the waterway to provide scenic views and access. Therefore, we must destroy the upland shore land vegetation and shallow water vegetation to provide view and access.

In our present perspective the forces of development often happen slowly and its effects on the natural world even more slowly. A person moves from his childhood surroundings in the city and returns twenty years later and is quick to recognize the developments in the non-natural world; but does not recognize the subtle changes that have occurred in the natural world. Why is this?

To recognize the loss of a fish species from a stream, the replacement of a native plant with an exotic in a meadow, or that a bird's song is missing from the air we must have an association with what was there originally. If we never recognized these things when they were in our presence, how do we recognize them in their absence? We have created an urbanized society so absent from nature that we feel we have been released from our responsibility towards it. It is time to awaken from the spell of progress by understanding our place in land time, not man's time.

The Land Trust

An increasingly important method of land conservation is a land trust that gives protection to land from uses that would otherwise destroy its natural attributes. Yet at the present there is no infrastructure that places trust in the land that realizes man's dependence on it.

Early man's religion and life centered on both fear and respect for nature or the land. Human dependence on the land was obvious in pioneer days when any act that ignored nature could mean death. Today this action-reaction to nature is not as obvious as technology and culture have cushioned us from the forces of nature and placed land at greater than arm's length. Today we are a mobile society that can ignore seasonal changes by traveling away from it. Modern society views nature and the land through windows we call natural disasters. As humanitarians we take social and political actions to alleviate the effects of its power and destruction. For example, international food production and distribution hides the effects of droughts, storms, and freezes that produce mass crop loss. Economic aid covers the wounds with a bandage while the effects of these disasters on the destruction of plant and animals' ecosystems is quickly forgotten.

Under these circumstances we will not recognize any global climatic changes hidden by the complexity of nature and the ignorance of industrialized man. The search for causes of land disasters is stymied by our attitude to react to short term situations and not long-term effects. By not paying attention to the lessons of the past we create accelerated disasters in the future. Our world spends millions of dollars on reacting to disaster and many more millions to produce crops to feed those effected by starvation, yet the most severe droughts take place where man had used and abused the land the longest. When will we recognize that changes in the world landscape will continue to increase the frequency and severity of natural disasters?

Time repeats itself so does the actions of man. Just as early man did, we place trust in gods and country, but we do not realize –

as early man did - that god and country is expressed most in those things in nature that we can see and feel. Trust is an action of faith that ensures that something will be here tomorrow without a worry that it will be influenced by change. We cannot commit ourselves to a faith until we can understand and feel it. With this faith comes the virtues of ethics. This is not the circumstances today. We no longer as a population see and feel nature, therefore it will continue to disappear. We take steps to conserve the land but there are bigger opposite actions that destroy what is being gained.

In this complicated world we continually seek solace from it. Finding a quiet place to take the time to reflect on one's place in it is getting more difficult as technology engulfs the human mind. Religion and nature are rebounding as refuges from this hectic world but where is the connection between the two that will create a reverence towards the land. Where is the movement that recognizes the importance of the integrity of the land in our survival?

The secret to finding progress towards this combination is to find a bridge between science and religion. This bridge is the true understanding of nature or the land. We need to create an educational process that can first recognize and then limit technological advances to those that maintain the integrity of the land. Those advances that can stand besides, be mixed with, and even restore what we have lost. A system that is universal to every action. This new attitude must have its upbringing in the reverence of youth wonder, influence, and discipline just as the young are exposed to the rites of the world religions.

What type of eternal infrastructure can we create to promote this as a worldwide point of view? I believe it must be a separate focus whose foundation needs to be built with natural science education but brought together in an environment of awe. It needs to stimulate the senses that allow it to be carried to the mind. It needs to carry the unknown overwhelming peace felt in the wilderness to a tranquility that comes with the understanding of interconnectedness. It needs to transfer the integrity of our personal wilderness to everyday ethics in the developments and technologies of man.

Overtime, this renewed human mindset will, again, recognize man's limit in nature. With this recognition will come solutions to ecological problems. Today wilderness advocates wonder how to solve the influences of too many visits to it or if there will be enough wilderness for an ever-increasing population. Tomorrow we could lose the definition of wilderness and wild in a presence of biodiversity closer to us. Many will be satisfied to stand at the edge that is all around us.

One must be optimistic that this collaboration will come about. Man can look at his destiny as a stark and bleak desert and lose all hope of survival ... or he can look at his past for solution to his land problems and connect the thinking mind to what is right. A land trust that is defined today in legal terms is nothing but a cog in a mighty social mechanism that we must create to survive.

The Resource Virtue

There are many lines being drawn between progress and preservation. The for-profit organizations draw lines in the name of economics as the non- profit organizations often draw lines for ecology. There is a wide line between these fine lines that government conservation operates in. All three have their own virtue that they tote with pride.

The wide line of government conservation often takes the form of written words. There are many names for these written words: manual codes, administrative codes, zoning ordinances, environmental law, or natural resource law. They are meant to bring an effective power of force to protect or use our resources wisely. Yet it appears today these laws are drawn in gray where politics and power hold the hand on the pencil- changing the definition or original intent of the law. The laws are created by those that try to widen the law line towards their side whether it is for progress or preservation. They use the politicians that are hungry for input from their constituents yet look for self-preservation with an open hand or a back-room deal. The time of those whose job it is to enforce the law is now spent on playing in their own gray political issues ... areas of public acceptance and/or administrative acceptance. For many, protection of the resources is in the field, where it counts, has become second to this conservation mastodon. The policy makers in conservation today are so removed from the land their decisions are not made with insight that man is part of the landscape and depends upon it for life.

While time passes in offices, rotundas, and courtrooms few note or understand the change in the landscape. No one has the time to observe the back forty as we are too busy making a dollar or defending our neighborhood against other people. What is the nature of these virtues that drive us?

We evolved from the land as hunters and gathers and our food, shelter and clothing were a result of our relatives or clan members producing these items for our survival. The integrity of the clan depended on the group working together and held together by tradition and custom. Their reverence to the land was closely tied to survival as well as these traditions and customs. There very being was to be part of the land. There was plenty for all.

As modern man increased his number, so he increased his mechanized society. Yet some remained closer to the land and others moved away from the land. The dependence on the land remained but the tradition and customs that held them together was lost in competition and by distance. Migration for survival had begun as well as the erosion of a land morality.

To feed and transport those removed from the land required leaps and bounds in technology and mass changes in the landscape. This race towards expansion of mankind was fierce until we mechanized to a point where free time was available. It is ironic that the instinct of early man's morality towards the land was sparked by the free time to use the senses that are common to all the animal world.

Yet on our return to nature, we have insisted on bringing the mechanical world with us. We insist that we must make our land experience return faster and easier. We must have the latest gadgets that the sporting industry can provide and use them in competition. What we miss is viewing the land with a critical eye, as the noise we create and the speed we travel only blurs the image our senses of instinct want to see.

The love of the machine is not unlike what we need to develop with the land again. The mechanic falls in love with his machine by understanding it. This understanding comes about by being alone with it, recognizing something is wrong with it, taking it apart, replacing the broken parts, and putting back together again. The smooth-running result creates a passion knowing that the right action has been taken to fix the problem and pride when he keeps it running smoothly.

Where are we in this process? Have we even recognized there is something wrong with the land machine? Government conservation tries to save the land machine through acquisition and stopping man's consumptive use of it. Preservationists want to idle the landscape machine and have man hover above it as a deity. The industrialist pushes the landscape machine for all its worth until all the parts are worn and broken, and replacement is impossible.

But is anyone working towards developing an understanding of and passion for the land machine? Is anyone being trained to recognize the intricacies of this natural machine and at the same time developing the capabilities of keeping it running smoothly? We need to create an educational approach and system to do this. We need to be alone with the land without the outside noises and influences and take this new route back towards the land.

We need to create a Planet Earth discipline that recognizes the broken parts; inventories the foreign parts that do not belong; understands the interaction of the working parts; and places them together for a smooth operation. This process will create great rewards in new ways.

We cannot do this without developing the power of observation of nature at an early age. Local community buildings need to be utilized as interpretive center for the soils, plants, and animals that can endure on the landscape with our help and conscious efforts. We must believe in and practice this landscape ecology approach and incorporate it into every action that involves the land in that community. The line between progress and preservation will someday be a line of survival based on our maintaining the integrity of the land.

This Planet of Whole Life

We see this Planet Earth as a place where our homes exist on continents and islands or for the more adventurous the iconic sailor, the seas. It is the sailor who is more attuned to this planet as he sees more of the interactions of life daily but is always happy to see land once and awhile. This being a planet of water the organisms of it equally are entities of this vital substance in every way; nevertheless, it is the wholeness that makes life on this planet Earth.

There are many founders of ecological thinking. Each had their own way of stating things in their own moments of ah ha! But one thing is certain even though they studied only one part of a defined ecosystem, they knew in their hearts there was, but one great system of matter and energy connected by water on this planet. So goes the continents and islands, where would they be without the seas of water around them!

The world of science is filled with knowledge of living organisms including individual species from single cells to the great blue whale; from individual plants to communities of the same; from combinations of minute microorganisms to ecosystems of tens of thousands of species. Yet all this knowledge and academic study does not indicate we know how the great system of the biosphere of Earth truly functions with the complicated interdependent connections between all.

The actions of thinking man have always led to progress in both knowledge and invention. The use of simple sticks and stones of our primitive ancestors was the beginning of engineering thought. At the same time the need for food created a penchant for the study of plant and animals, thus biological science of discovery evolved. These beginnings have grown to many specialties, then to combined professions of specialties, and in the complexities of life have now created divisions.

Engineers divide into many specialties: civil, chemical, electrical, mechanical, and nuclear. Each creating some functioning tool to extract or create something from this Planet Earth and make life easier for humans. These great focuses of development and success has taken a great toll on this planet that now fosters the field of environmental engineering ... which seems to create a recognition between development and nature, which I hope has not come too late.

The world of biology and chemistry combined with engineering has splintered into hundreds of specialties lead by man's well-being as a focus. Our advances in creating chemical compounds and objects made from earth's resources and used by billions of people has created not only a stream of unusable waste but earth, water, and air problems effecting all living things on earth. Today it has evolved to a point that our technological advances and progress is causing many, if not most, of our health problems.

What biologist have not done is to connect the dots of what once held the functioning earth together and prevented the loss of many dots. Biologist now, theoretically, are saying we can live without some of the dots and recognize other dots as keys to intact ecosystems. Yet, even unknown dots are vanishing as we have no collective data base to even make connections of the known let alone the important similarities of what we do not know or understand. We must recognize that understanding the ecology of the dots, all living organisms, and their connections are man's blueprint for survival of all organisms on this earth ... including humans. A mega database is the beginning of a human insight connecting the scientific world to an ethical one.

Every year microbiologist and biochemist are making discoveries that explain the intricacies of the microscopic world that makes the macroscopic world that man sees with human eyes possible. They are finding the complexities of life created through billions of years of evolution have connections that makes all life a coordinated function. Man tries to justify protection of endangered species on the grounds that someday this organism might harbor the key to some undiscovered element that might be a cure for man's woes, such as cancer. Where this may be true as we justify saving it as a benefit to humans, but if we lose a species which has an ecosystem role, we also loose the genetic viability of biological diversity that cannot be replicated in a future, when we find it is important to all living existence. We will continue to depend on the variety of life for food, clothing, and medicines in the future so we must be adamant in making sure all the components that make life function are in place.

Can we learn lessons from the plight of endangered species? Might we compare a species of flower to the many human races that encompass the planet. According to the Convention on International Trade in Endangered Species (CITIES) list there are over thirty thousand endangered species. About twenty-four thousand are orchids. Humans are unique as orchids and are found all over the world, but many are concentrated in the tropics. Orchids and humans are needy early in life. Both species produce an abundance of offspring, but both species are helpless at birth, as orchid seeds have no energy storage as does a newborn child.

Which specie should we have more empathy for when survival is in jeopardy?

Many endangered plants have specific requirements in both the soil and hydrology of a geological landscape. Where habitat destruction was the broad category to the reasons for losses of both of endangered plants and animals', climate change and global warming is a new general threat with a new kind of twist. Entire plant communities, because of climate change, are shifting north and south in both hemispheres, respectively.

What will happen to the endangered plants and animals that are dependent on the hydrology and geological features that are not present in the new landscape? Extinction? What are human specific requirements for survival on earth?

Has this happened before? I expect it has. Yet do we need to preserve the species "in situ"(in their original places) or by artificial propagation? To be successful at this is exceedingly difficult, but an understanding to culture anything has always been a pride in botany, agronomy, and plant genetics. So then, do we preserve a species with reason or without a reason? Does a plant or animal struggling on this earth deserve preservation even through artificial propagation just because it exists? I say yes. We morally have an obligation to preserve all life just as we cherish human life. But how do we do this with the great cost involved when there are humans fighting the same battles? Perhaps the answers are the same, eventually the saving of both will depend on the saving of each other. The food- water- shelter basis in a limited world will become dependent upon the efficiencies of the diverse world that was created from the beginning of time and our ability to apply these same efficiencies to the future.

Again, we must point to what will save nature? Will it be the land and species that evolved through time that we evolved with? Will it be laws or ethics that will prevail in this time of man? Natural laws are the rules in which human instinct and feelings dictate whereas positive law are rules established by courts, legislatures, resolves and other bodies whose task is to resolve conflict between individuals and an establish order for society. Are our instincts and feeling no longer relevant as the laws that are interpreted and resolved by prejudices that favor industry, commerce, and communities that ultimately will destroy nature? I vote for an education that creates a society and world view that all species are important, and their preservation is the preservation of all. Ethically, humans must limit his actions and consumption that destroy nature and use his knowledge and technology to reverse the adverse impact he has already caused this Planet Earth. We must go forward with a land ethic that endures and brightens our possibility for a continuing life on Earth.

We are entering a time that wealth and power threaten the knowledge of nature that someday will be what saves man from himself. We must study nature, all the animals, plants, and micro species, so that we might understand their part in the survival of all. Currently, if we have identified their survival is in jeopardy, we have created laws to protect and restore it, but the funds to do this can and are being eliminated and these former laws can be gutted in the political game of big industry and greed in America. At the same time, we push and pull for conservation and development in other areas of the world that threatens wilderness species and habitats that we are just beginning to study and understand. Our world economy and commerce movements pollute our oceans with plastics, residues of oil, and more contaminants that threatens the creatures and ecosystems of our vast oceans.

Who is collecting the vast knowledge of what is known of the ecology of all species before it fails and expansive collapses in ecosystems occur? Diseases and pandemics, famines and starvations, and battles that become wars, are signs of death of our species because we caused the death of other species.

We have many land conservation methods to try and save species. They seem to fall to three overlapping areas: Save large areas of habitat by purchase, placing conservation easements in hope to providing a buffer, and convincing private purchase of areas surrounding the critical habitat. Creating laws that protect the plant or animal species seem not to be that effective. In the past it has taken a minimum of 15 years of law processing in America to create a wilderness area. How much time do we have to save planet?

The purchasing of large areas of habitat or existing large areas in public protection are at the mercy of the political forces of time. If one looks at history, the economic conditions, whether in third world or the wealthiest countries, seem to affect the effectiveness of this protection.

The protection of the megafauna of Africa is key to maintaining diversity. Wealthy trophy hunters for more than five centuries have killed rhinoceros, elephants, and great apes for horns, ivory tusk, and even hands now endanger these key species at the top of the food pyramid. Poaching, starvation, and war also have riddled hope for the preservation of habitat that can save the pristine ecosystems that support these animals. Biological preserves do little good when humans have little food and greed and power separate those that have and those who do not.

In America, the foresight of our ancestors has create vast public parks, forests, natural, areas, and wilderness areas as icons of conservation. Today these icons are constantly feeling the pressure of use by the ever-increasing population. These refuges of conservation in America were new ideas to this planet Earth. There is a current move to stop resource extraction on public lands. We can only hope it happens.

But man's impact on this natural world is so overwhelming and from so many different angles of assaults the ecological understanding has not kept up. Conservation has become so political that both private and government are at the hands of money and corporate institutions. The nations who have created wealth through the unwise use and destruction of their resources are now using this wealth and power to exploit the resources of third world countries while at the same time to improve their standard of living. Has not humanity learned that this imperialism and globalization continues to destroy sustaining resources?

No nation on this planet can thrive today without understanding its own resources which includes an ecological understanding.

This understanding includes its own history and its own ethical utilizing its resources without destroying the air, water, and land that it comes from. Wealthy nations must recognize this in poorer nations, then provide ecological guidance with an equity that does not destroy its culture or land.

A collection of ecological knowledge of all species needs to be collected and maintained. It should be used to make decisions that preserves the integrity of intact and disturbed ecosystem communities in both undeveloped and developed countries. Computers today can create a mega database that connect all we know of species relationships to each other and their ecosystem role. This system can be shared with cultures and governments for the wise use and development of their resources; for those, whose natural resources have been severely disrupted or destroyed, it can be used for their restoration.

To Die While Living

There is a popular point of view that humans can abuse the Earth and as a planet it will adjust. Contrary to this contemporary juxtaposition - as with the dinosaurs, man will be gone. The earth will continue spinning around the sun, creating matter out of carbon, nitrogen, and oxygen. Humanity is leaving our children this disposition unless we can mature to an ethic that knows the land and treats it as it is their own child.

We have come to a point where we teach children about the connection between the air, sun, plants, and soil through the story of photosynthesis. But, as we tell them how a tree sprouts and grows should we be telling them that humans are killing the trees through too much nitrogen, acid, or carbon dioxide? That the trees we are killing are the original trees that survived the great glaciers, that produced the seeds that spread and replanted the forest as the glacier retreated? Perhaps stir their imaginations by telling them a story that now we can create conditions for a tree that looks alive but falls over, seemingly without warning, just as grandpa did when he has a massive heart attack. We can spend a lifetime understanding what makes things grow but fail to prevent what makes things die- even when we know the cause.

We live in a competitive world that we have reacted to with fear. We consider America among the most advanced country as defined by our high standard of living and persistence of personal freedoms. But with these high ideals, comes an unconscious need to maintain them at any cost. Education is our key to our competition. Our standards of reading, writing, and mathematics are geared to meet goals of a high standard of living, not an understanding of the world around us. If our education were to train our children to truly identify our place in a biological community, the perception of personal freedom would change. Life would have more meaning and the definition of 'competition' would always include the concepts of ecology and a relationship to land that we would understand and respect.

When one recognizes a problem with the environment often it is invisible to the common person of today. Air pollution or acid rain is not visible unless you see it at the point of release in a smokestack, in an untuned dump truck, or under the right light conditions in populated areas that have smog. The nose is often the first sense to tell us something is wrong if you happen to be down wind. But who can see what makes a tree die? If we take a moment, what we may see is the fungus on the bark, invading insects on the trunk or leaves, or several woodpecker holes. Most of these observations are nature reacting to the dying of the tree by other causes - only a few of which are natural. In winter, the dead branches are more visible. In summer, much death begins in the upper reaches -farthest from the roots; the death above remains hidden by the green foliage between you on the ground. If we are not a forester or arborist, we are not capable of determining these discreet differences may be due to acid rain. But if you are a sugar bush owner who has spent a lifetime making a living off the syrup developed in the crown you would notice! We can be trained in youth to slow down and notice ... and to question why of the causes and effects through a lifetime.

If we fail to develop a spiritual connection with nature, a compassion that comes through knowledge, understanding, and emotion, are we not slowly dying? Our forests are slowly dying; we do not recognize the problem because we can only see the now with the unconscious eye of the immediate returns. The death of a plant community - however slow - foretells the death of what is beneath and what is above.

To Think Like Einstein

The life of Einstein was a drama that is being acted out today .... but we do not realize its potential in solving today's problems: His genius could be found within his passion for knowledge of the unknown; his determination in the face of scholarly and political strife; and his abilities to focus on and comprehend complex concepts while putting them into simpler words for explanation's sake.

A few years ago, there was a saying "We need to think out of the box". It was on everyone's lips in every discipline. It meant we need creative thought beyond the current practices and norms. It seemed to be a passing phrase and has become a cliché. What prevents you thinking beyond the thoughts and recognitions of others?   I believe the human mind could take all of mankind's collective knowledge and express it in new ways.

The experts on the brain at one time believed that humans only utilized ten percent of its capacity. But now we are finding that we use it for so much more. The brain often blocks memories. Yes, life gets in the way ... even when we are not aware of it. As young babies, and perhaps even before we are born (in our genetic history) and long before we have memories, we may have had watershed moments that create blocking mechanisms in our mental development.

How often do you suddenly remember some instance in your past that you long forgot? How often do you have dreams, if you do remember them, that you know you were present ... but not there? How many of us trust our subconscious to solve problems? Do problems keep you from going to sleep or do you fall asleep quickly and the solution to the problem appears the next morning after a deep sleep? Our mind is a wonderful thing, why waste it.

How would you change your life if you really knew your brain is capable to retain and sort out all the knowledge you have acquired through time ... and you could act upon this ability to make this a better world? We know those that have a photographic or identic memory that easily repeat what they have observed or read; however, to take this information and sort it into a useful purpose to make good decisions to help humanity understand this Planet Earth and beyond is the probably the true definition of genius.

If there ever was a time when this genius was needed, it would be now. The power of knowledge and intelligence needs new ways to face the problems and politics of our time. There is a divide between the people that are educated ... perhaps too educated for their own good ... and those who do not give creed to knowledge and the information man creates to make decisions. A wise friend of mine said the other day "We have politicians and people who lead our country that say, 'I do not know about that, but it must be right' and they are serious." It is sad, that in this digital information age where media could inform all in every way imaginable that this has happened. Yet the ivory towers of the informed are filled with experts in the narrow focus on one subject; and the uninformed scoff at this professional elitism that has not solved the world problems.

This is a time for an action that can pull all together. This is a time for those who have given up or say things are hopeless to see something that can make changes that all mankind can see and benefit from. We need to take the complex knowledge we have of living things and make sense of it all, connect the dots of what makes life function. We need to take our brains capacity to a new level by using it with computer mega data and take the collective data of man's knowledge of living things to a new level of global action.

This new level of data will create knowledge of interconnections that will give a base and backbone to conclusions; good choices will follow that will solve major problems our Planet Earth is facing. This mega data base can now be used to unfold the complexes of nature into concepts for all to understand and follow with informed decisions that people can respect and support.

What We Need to Do

This is what we need to do. This Planet Earth is a complex place. We need to understand the relationship between all living organisms. Air, water, food, and a healthy environment is vital to all. Studying individual species is impossible as we only have recognized about 20%. But we need to understand the connections between the organisms we have studied and documented; this will lead in a direction of what we need to do to preserve all. Every organism on this planet has a physical, chemical, and biological connection that allows it to grow, reproduce, and survive. In this computer age we have ability to identify these connections. Once we do this a web of life will emerge that will help identify what we need to do to preserve and protect this complex Planet Earth.

Why establish this data base? The twenty percent of living organisms we have identified through nomenclature are the species we have research data on. These are living things man has interacted with... and affected. These are ones we have studied as individuals but not understood fully their place in ecosystems and their coalitions with other organisms. Many of the other eighty percent are in areas of the world undiscovered, untouched, or remote to the direct actions of man, yet are affected by manmade actions taking place on the global scale in our oceans and atmosphere. We need this data base to recognize the connections and balances of a global ecosystem.

How do we establish this data base? Metanalysis, a tabulation of combined data from multiple studies to analyze them as one data set. A massive collection of biological, physical, and chemical knowledge brought together in a computer network to create a web of connections between all living things.

What are the benefits? This web of connections would be a base for corrective guides to understanding of life forces on earth and on possibly another planet in the future. It would create a guide to decisions on saving ecosystem collapses by identifying connecting components. A range of inventories of major species do exist (e.g.,

Map of Life) but a greater inventory of all life and its ecology would give justification to pinpointing and characterizing serious problems caused by climate change or overuse or depletion of certain natural resources. But most important of all we need to have a good basis to make decisions for a new field of what I call "true ecological restoration". Without a system that identifies every component of individual species and ecosystem interconnections the process of identifying and repairing disruptions will be faced with a great many failures and time lost to poor decisions and actions.

What are the implications? The world of science is now filled with taking details of studies out of context and making claims whether it be in academia or industry. The theoretical and modeling world of biodiversity and ecosystem management needs a base to launch good decisions on the land and sea. Understanding the relationship between plants, animals, and microorganisms that we have identified in context of the total ecology of the earth is essential in making good decisions for our survival. Economic development in third world countries can utilize this information in utilizing their resources without destroying them. We can no longer just consider our own human importance but must focus on all living organisms, including those we are not aware of ... and care for them as we would for our own children.

About the Author

Rand Atkinson is an ecologist, professor, environmental consultant, fish farmer, and a passionate seeker of knowledge about the natural world. This life-long adventure and accumulation of awareness of what is happening to the world he loves has created this book of concern and direction.

Rand graduated as a field biologist at the beginning of the 1970's environmental movement and quickly became immersed in water law, ecological assessments, and a need how to feed the world responsibly. With his passion of following Aldo Leopold's land ethics started companies to evaluate and restore aquatic systems, rear native plants, and grow fish sustainably. Eventually, he has passed his knowledge as an adjunct professor in restoration and reclamation.

Rand currently resides in the Northwoods of Wisconsin where he can observe and enjoy "the land" just out the door of his cabin. From here he continues to seek and write about the intersection of nature and humankind ... with hope!

Rand Atkinson

raferndockpublishing@gmail.com

A.L. Ferndock Publishing LLC
R.A.Ferdock, Publisher
3894 Star Lake Road
Star Lake WI 54561
Phone; 608-778-1131
raferndockpublishing@gmail.com

HOW TO ORDER & CONTACT US

Telephone & Text Orders:

Call or Text 608-778-1131 w/ info below.

Email Orders & Online Orders Venmo:

AL Ferndock

<u>raferndockpublishing@gmail.com</u>

A.L. Ferndock Publishing LLC
R.A.Ferdock, Publisher
3894 Star Lake Road
Star Lake WI 54561
Phone; 608-778-1131
raferndockpublishing@gmail.com

Number of Copies: _____ x $24.99 =$_____

Sales Tax: (5.5% for WI) = $_____

Shipping: ($4.00 for first book, $2.00 Add'l)

= $_____

Name_____Phone_____

Mailing Address_____

City_____State_____Zip____

Make checks payable to A.L. Ferndock Publishing LLC, or pay by debit or credit card with the information below: Circle Card Name & Type (Visa or MasterCard)
VS ___ MC ___ AX ___ DS ___ Check Enclosed ___

Card #_____Exp.Date_____

Name_____ 3-Digit Security Code_____